DATE DUE

6519

Metro Litho
Oak Forest, IL 60452

SEP 21 1992			

AMERICA the BEAUTIFUL

WEST VIRGINIA

By R. Conrad Stein

Consultants

Rodney S. Collins, Historian, West Virginia Division of Culture and History

Douglas J. Walters, Director of Staff Development, Kanawha County Schools, Charleston

Robert L. Hillerich, Ph.D., Bowling Green State University, Bowling Green, Ohio

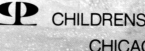

CHILDRENS PRESS®
CHICAGO

Holly River, Holly River State Park

Project Editor: Joan Downing
Associate Editor: Shari Joffe
Design Director: Margrit Fiddle
Typesetting: Graphic Connections, Inc.
Engraving: Liberty Photoengraving

Library of Congress Cataloging-in-Publication Data

Stein, R. Conrad.
  America the beautiful. West Virginia / by
R. Conrad Stein.
    p.   cm.
  Includes index.
  Summary: Discusses the geography, history,
people, government, economy, and recreation of
West Virginia.
   ISBN 0-516-00494-8
   1. West Virginia—Juvenile literature.
[1. West Virginia] I. Title.
F241.3.S74 1990   90-33848
975.4—dc20   CIP
                                 AC

The moon over Seneca Rocks

TABLE OF CONTENTS

Chapter 1
ALMOST HEAVEN

ALMOST HEAVEN

> Almost heaven, West Virginia,
> Blue Ridge Mountains, Shenandoah River,
> Life is old there, older than the trees,
> Younger than the mountains, growing like a breeze.

These lines open a charming song called "Take Me Home, Country Roads," made famous by singer John Denver. But are the lines an overstatement? Is West Virginia really "almost heaven"? Ask the coal miner who faces nagging unemployment, as did his father and no doubt his grandfather. Ask the teacher who earns far less than teachers in most other states. Ask, and you might receive a curious answer: "Yes, West Virginia is 'almost heaven.'"

There are many reasons why, despite its problems, people love West Virginia. One reason is the land. So lovely is the state that it has been called the Switzerland of America. The people are another reason why West Virginia is revered. West Virginians pride themselves on being friendly, honest, and straightforward.

The state also has a proud past. It was born amid the fire and fury of the Civil War. It was home to many American luminaries, including frontier trailblazer Daniel Boone, Civil War general Thomas "Stonewall" Jackson, educator Booker T. Washington, and novelist Pearl S. Buck.

West Virginia is nicknamed the Mountain State, and its people are called Mountaineers. Through the years, West Virginians have labored to keep true the state's bold motto: *Montani Semper Liberi* (Mountaineers Are Always Free).

Chapter 2
THE LAND

THE LAND

*[In West Virginia] rough mountains rise
all about. . . . On gray days they are
heavy and sullen, but on summer mornings
they are dizzy with color.*
—James M. Cain, from *These United States* (1924)

GEOGRAPHY

West Virginia has been called the most western of the eastern
states and the most eastern of the western states. Also, some
people refer to it as the most southern of the northern states,
while others claim it is the most northern of the southern states.
When geographers use the term "border state," West Virginia
comes instantly to mind.

The Mountain State has an odd shape, looking somewhat like a
frog with its two hind legs in a full back kick. The two "legs" are
the Northern and Eastern panhandles. It is the only state with two
panhandles. An old joke is told about its irregular configuration:
"West Virginia's a pretty fine state, considering the shape it's in."

Five states border West Virginia: Ohio, Kentucky, Virginia,
Maryland, and Pennsylvania. Most of its boundary lines are
formed by rivers or mountain peaks. In the northwest, the Ohio
River separates West Virginia from the state of Ohio. To the
southwest, the Big Sandy and Tug Fork rivers make up West
Virginia's border with Kentucky and a small portion of Virginia.

West Virginia, with its rugged hills and mountains, is aptly named the Mountain State.

Mountain peaks complete the eastern border with Virginia. The Potomac River along the northern and eastern borders of the Eastern Panhandle forms the state's boundary with Maryland. The Northern Panhandle is a long, narrow wedge of land driven between the states of Ohio and Pennsylvania.

Spreading over 24,231 square miles (62,758 square kilometers), West Virginia is forty-first in size among the states. Charleston is West Virginia's capital and its largest city.

THE MOUNTAIN STATE

Even a casual visitor realizes at once how West Virginia earned its nickname the Mountain State. From skyline to skyline, hills and mountains rise like waves in a choppy sea. There is scarcely a square mile of flat land anywhere. Some geographers have calculated that if West Virginia's endless mountains were

Spruce Knob, in the Appalachian Ridge and Valley region, is the state's highest point.

miraculously ironed out, its area would eclipse that of the continental United States.

West Virginia is made up of three land regions: the Appalachian Ridge and Valley, the Appalachian Plateau, and the Blue Ridge. In the Appalachian Ridge and Valley region, the state's tallest mountains—the Alleghenies—rise majestically along the eastern border with Virginia. In this region is the state's highest point, Spruce Knob, at 4,863 feet (1,482 meters) above sea level.

West of the Alleghenies' peaks spreads a rugged land region called the Appalachian Plateau. This plateau covers about 80 percent of the state's area and holds most of its population. West Virginia's largest deposits of coal, oil, natural gas, and salt are also found in this region.

At the eastern tip of the state's Eastern Panhandle stand the lovely Blue Ridge Mountains, part of the Appalachian chain. The

The New River, in the southern part of the state

fertile valley of the Shenandoah River, which runs through the Blue Ridge region, provides rich soil for apple and peach orchards.

Aside from their rugged beauty, the mountains have been a two-edged sword in West Virginia's history. Beneath the mountains lie the state's vital natural resources: coal, natural gas, oil, clay, sand, and gravel. But the towering mountains make much of the state's land area difficult or impossible to farm. West Virginia's agricultural yield is one of the poorest in the fifty states.

RIVERS AND LAKES

The mightiest river within the state's borders is the Kanawha, which starts at the meeting of the Gauley and New rivers and empties into the Ohio. The Elk, Coal, and Pocatalico rivers run into the Kanawha as it flows toward the Ohio. Other West Virginia tributaries of the Ohio in the western part of the state

Summersville Lake is one of the state's largest reservoirs.

include Fishing Creek, Mill Creek, the Little Kanawha, the
Guyandotte, and the Big Sandy.

To the north is the Monongahela River and its branches: the
Cheat, Tygart, and West Fork rivers. Flowing north into
Pennsylvania, the Monongahela, along with the Allegheny River,
forms the Ohio River at Pittsburgh.

In the Eastern Panhandle, the Shenandoah, Back Creek, and
Cacapon rivers flow north into the Potomac River. The New River
and the Greenbrier are scenic rivers in the southern part of the
state.

The Mountain State has no large natural lakes. Artificial lakes,
or reservoirs, have been created by dams built along the state's
river systems. Summersville Lake and Sutton Lake, both located in
the central part of the state, are two of the largest reservoirs.

Maple trees (above) and rare wild plants such as sundews (left) are native to the state.

PLANTS AND ANIMALS

Hundreds of years ago, almost all of West Virginia was covered by magnificent forests. Forest fires and the work of loggers and pioneer farmers wiped out those once-towering woods. Today, however, second-growth and later-growth trees cover about four-fifths of the state. Evergreen forests of white pine, red spruce, and hemlock rise on the mountain slopes and on the riverbanks. Cherry and oak are the most common hardwood trees.

Lovers of wildflowers delight in taking nature walks along West Virginia's mountain paths. A lucky hiker may sight rare plants such as bog rosemary, coltsfoot, and sundews. Azaleas, kalmias, and rhododendrons are common shrubs in the Mountain State.

White-tailed deer and black bears are among
the animals that live in West Virginia.

Deer, black bears, gray and red foxes, raccoons, opossums,
minks, and skunks inhabit West Virginia's forests. At one time,
wastes from mines and sawmills destroyed many of the state's
game fish, but a conservation effort has given new life to the
rivers. Walleye, bass, and trout are now common in the
waterways. West Virginia is a nesting ground for more than three
hundred species of birds, including wrens, cardinals, and scarlet
tanagers. Some unusual birds include eagles, hawks, great horned
owls, ruffed grouse, and wild turkeys.

CLIMATE

West Virginia enjoys gentle weather that features warm, humid
summers and mild winters. Even in mid-January, long periods of
below-freezing temperatures are unusual. In most cases, the river
valleys are warmer than the mountain peaks. The average July
high temperature in Charleston, located in a river valley, is 87
degrees Fahrenheit (31 degrees Celsius), while Elkins, in the
mountains, has an average high July temperature of 83 degrees

16

Even though West Virginia's climate is generally mild, several inches of snow falls during the winter.

Fahrenheit (28 degrees Celsius). West Virginia's mountain areas experience the coldest average January temperatures of 22 degrees Fahrenheit (minus 6 degrees Celsius). The state's southern region's average low January temperature is about 27 degrees Fahrenheit (minus 3 degrees Celsius).

The Eastern Panhandle has a moderate coastal climate because it is not far from the Atlantic Ocean. Sometimes, however, West Virginia is subject to extremes of weather. The thermometer reached 112 degrees Fahrenheit (44 degrees Celsius) at Moorefield on August 4, 1930, and it dropped to minus 37 degrees Fahrenheit (minus 38 degrees Celsius) at Lewisburg on December 30, 1917.

An average of 45 to 50 inches (114 to 127 centimeters) of total precipitation (rain, sleet, and snow) falls on West Virginia each year. While drought is rarely a problem, flash floods sometimes ravage towns in the river valleys. Snowfall is highest on the mountaintops, where the snow can drift 5 feet (1.5 meters) high or more. Snowfall each year ranges from 20 inches (51 centimeters) in the southwest to as much as 100 inches (254 centimeters) in the central and northeastern mountains.

17

Chapter 3
THE PEOPLE

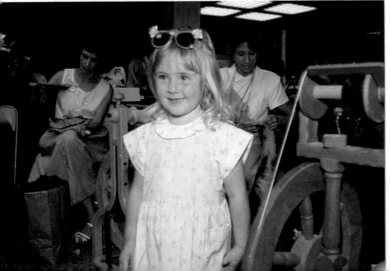

THE PEOPLE

Great things are done when men and mountains meet.
—William Blake, an English poet

POPULATION AND POPULATION DISTRIBUTION

The 1980 census counted 1,950,258 people living in West Virginia. This was a 12 percent increase over the 1970 population figure. The surge in population was heralded by West Virginians as a sign of prosperity. For the previous two decades, a chronic lack of jobs had driven many working-class families out of the state. The population dropped from 2 million in 1950 to 1.7 million in 1970. However, estimated 1990 census figures indicate that Mountaineers are once more looking for job opportunities elsewhere. West Virginia is expected to be one of only seven states to have lost population between 1980 and 1990.

The Mountain State is one of the few American states in which a majority of the people reside in rural communities. Nationwide, only one of every four Americans live in rural areas, but in West Virginia two of every three residents are rural dwellers. Small coal-mining towns are common in the state, and account for most of the large rural population.

Charleston, in the south-central part of the state, is West Virginia's largest city, with 63,968 people. The Ohio River city of Huntington is a close second, with 63,684 people. Wheeling, a

Most West Virginia residents were born in the United States.

steel-mill center that lies in the Northern Panhandle, is the third-largest city, with 43,070 people. Jefferson County, in the tip of the Eastern Panhandle, is home to many commuters who work in the Washington, D.C., area.

WHO ARE THE MOUNTAINEERS?

Since early in the twentieth century, few immigrants from foreign countries have settled in West Virginia. Consequently, almost all Mountaineers today were born in the United States. Among the white population, English and German backgrounds are most common. Many West Virginians also have Irish and Italian ancestors. About 3 percent of West Virginians are black. Less than 1 percent are of Hispanic heritage. There are about 1,600

This restored nineteenth-century Pioneer Farm in Twin Falls State Park
is a reminder that many Mountaineers can trace their ancestry to the pioneers.

Native Americans and small numbers of Asian Indians, Filipinos,
Chinese, Koreans, Japanese, and Vietnamese.

Many West Virginians can trace their ancestry to the pioneers.
Villages in those frontier days were gathering places of family
groups that formed loose-knit clans. Annual clan reunions are
popular events in West Virginia today. Some clan get-togethers
attract thousands of loosely related people.

Many of the same family groups have remained in a village for
generations. A West Virginia doctor, while visiting out of state,
told of meeting a woman whose sister-in-law lived in the
Appalachian mountain community of Union. "I bet her name is
Wikel," said the doctor. The woman replied that indeed it was,
but how did he know? The doctor frowned, "Well, from Union, it
had to be either Wikel, or Parker, or Pence."

Baptists and Methodists are the largest religious groups in the state.

Methodists and Baptists are the largest church groups in the state. Many Mountaineers are fundamentalists, meaning they believe in a strict, literal interpretation of the Bible. Although the Disciples of Christ church originated in Pennsylvania, its beliefs spread throughout the country after the church moved to West Virginia. The state also saw the growth of early Seventh Day Baptist societies. The Roman Catholic, Presbyterian, and Evangelical United Brethren churches also have followings in West Virginia.

POLITICS

In the past, West Virginia's voters were solidly Democratic, but the Republican party made inroads in the 1980s. After the 1988 election, however, West Virginia's governor, both United States senators, and four representatives to Congress were all Democrats.

The state has a tradition of returning politicians to office for many terms. Democrat Jennings Randolph served more than forty

Cabin Creek, a few miles southeast of Charleston, is one of the state's many coal towns.

years in Congress before retiring in 1985. Democrat Robert C. Byrd, one of the United States senators in the 1990s, was first elected in 1958. Arch Moore, a Republican, served a record three terms as governor. Since 1936, West Virginians have given a majority of their votes to a Republican presidential candidate only three times—to reelect presidents Eisenhower, Nixon, and Reagan.

WAYS OF LIFE

New industries brought jobs and progress to West Virginia in the 1970s and the 1980s. But the legacy of poverty lingers. For decades, West Virginia, especially the Appalachian region, was one of the poorest areas in the United States. Grimy coal towns, violent labor wars, and bloody family feuds—such as the one between the Hatfields and the McCoys—have been bitter elements of the people's way of life.

Dependence on a single industry—coal—is central to the state's long bout with poverty. The coal industry suffers from a boom-or-bust price syndrome. When coal prices are high, people find work;

24

Even though new industries have grown in West Virginia, the lifestyles of many residents still depend on the price of coal. When prices are up, miners find work, but when prices drop, they lose their jobs.

when coal prices fall, they lose their jobs. After World War II, machines began to replace workers in the mines. Even in the 1980s—when the state's industry had diversified to lessen its reliance on coal—West Virginia's unemployment rate was three times the national average.

Today in West Virginia, visitors notice swarms of cars with Illinois, Michigan, and Ohio license plates. Many are driven by former Mountaineers who fled to those more industrialized states seeking jobs. West Virginia, it is said, is one of the nation's most popular places to be *from*.

When many Americans think of West Virginia, a certain negative stereotype comes to mind. They picture a redneck, or hillbilly, a shallow-minded white racist who cannot adjust to new ideas. West Virginians bristle at this image. "Hillbillies, they call us," said Don West, a West Virginia writer. "They don't remember that tens of thousands of southern Appalachian men volunteered for the Union in the Civil War. How many people know that one reason why West Virginia became a state was that the hillbillies rejected the idea of slavery?"

Chapter 4

THE BEGINNING

THE BEGINNING

Leave me but a banner to plant in the
mountains of [western Virginia], and I will
gather around me the men who will lift our bleeding
country from the dust and set her free.
—George Washington, a Virginia planter,
colonial leader, and president-to-be

THE FIRST WEST VIRGINIANS

About thirty-five thousand years ago, people from Asia began entering North America by crossing a land bridge that once existed in the Bering Strait. After a march that lasted thousands of years, their descendants pushed into the Appalachian region about 15,000 B.C. Those early people camped mostly in the river valleys, where they hunted mammoths, mastodons, camels, and other exotic Ice Age animals. Throughout the state, archaeologists have found tools and arrow tips left by those ancient residents. A large prehistoric campsite stood along the Ohio River near the present-day city of Parkersburg.

Eventually, the Native Americans who lived in the Appalachian region developed farming. Agriculture allowed the people to gather in more-or-less permanent villages. Farming gave them more leisure time to pursue arts and crafts.

Some three thousand years ago, the Native Americans, or Indian people, of what is now the eastern United States began

The Grave Creek Mound, in Moundsville, is the largest burial mound in the state.

constructing huge earthen mounds. The mounds were used either as burial sites or as centers of worship. More than three hundred mounds remain in West Virginia today. The largest is the Grave Creek Mound, which stands at the town of Moundsville. At South Charleston rises a mound that was the burial place of a giant. One of the skeletons excavated at the South Charleston mound was 7 feet, 6 inches (2.3 meters) tall.

For unknown reasons, mound building ceased around A.D. 500. Centuries later, when white settlers entered West Virginia, the once-impressive mounds were covered with trees and shrubs and looked much like the state's endless hills.

At the time of white settlement, the region that is now West Virginia held few permanent Indian residents. About a dozen Shawnee villages stood near Point Pleasant, and a scattering of Mingo and Tuscarora communities were strung out along the Potomac River in what is now the Eastern Panhandle. The Iroquois-speaking people to the north and the Algonquian-

At the time of white settlement, West Virginia was crisscrossed with dozens of Indian trails, including the Seneca Trail, which passed near Seneca Rocks (above).

speaking people to the east used the land primarily as a hunting ground. They found this land too rugged for year-round living.

The future state was crisscrossed with dozens of Indian trails. The most widely used footpath was the Seneca Trail (also called the Shawnee Trail), which passed through the present-day towns of Parsons, Elkins, Marlinton, Lewisburg, and Bluefield. Today, U.S. Route 219 closely follows the old Seneca Trail.

Almost unknown to the Indians who hunted in what is now
West Virginia were the developments in the flatlands east of the
Appalachian Mountains. There, in 1607, a handful of Englishmen
had established the colony of Virginia, which included the land of
present-day West Virginia. Virginia's colonists saw the Appalachian
peaks in the distance and dreamed that some day they would
bring English civilization to the land they called "the West."

THE EXPLORERS

Probably the first European to set eyes on West Virginia soil
was German geographer John Lederer. Between 1669 and 1670, he
undertook three expeditions to the West for Governor William
Berkeley of Virginia. On one of his trips, he reached the Blue
Ridge Mountains near the present West Virginia boundary line
and gazed down at the lovely Shenandoah Valley. Lederer saw
vast herds of elk. He also claimed that he saw a lake 30 miles
(48 kilometers) wide. But no such body of water existed then or
now in the Blue Ridge region.

A second exploration party, headed by Thomas Batts and Robert
Fallam, left Virginia and crossed the Appalachian Mountains in
1671. The group came upon the New River, which—to their
astonishment—flowed west. All other rivers in Virginia moved
east to empty into the Atlantic Ocean. The Batts-Fallam group
found another surprise when they saw several trees in the
Appalachians with the letters *MANI* clearly carved on their bark.
To this day, no one knows what the letters meant or who could
have put them on the trees of an unexplored forest.

Wealthy Englishman James Needham led an expedition into the
Appalachians in 1673. Needham hoped to open trade between
Virginia and the Cherokee nation to the south. Traveling with

Alexander Spotswood (above) led an expedition across the Blue Ridge Mountains in 1716 (left).

Needham was Gabriel Arthur, a young man who hungered for adventure. After making contact with the Cherokees, Needham returned to Virginia. Young Gabriel Arthur remained in the Indian camp. Cherokee warriors took Arthur on a hunting trip into the forests and mountains. While camped at the present-day city of St. Albans, Arthur became the first non-Indian to see the broad Kanawha Valley, which would later become West Virginia's heartland.

A true adventurer in the Mountain State's early history was Englishman Alexander Spotswood. While serving as lieutenant governor of Virginia, Spotswood led an expedition of discovery across the Blue Ridge Mountains in 1716. Upon returning, he gave each member of his group a tiny gold horseshoe. In modern times, the state government of West Virginia has awarded gold-colored horseshoes as prizes to students who have mastered the history of the Mountain State.

SETTLEMENT

The vast majority of western Virginia's earliest settlers came not
from Virginia, but from the colonies of Pennsylvania, New York,
New Jersey, Delaware, and Maryland. Men and women from
those eastern colonies moved first to the Eastern Panhandle. One
of western Virginia's earliest permanent settlers was a Welsh
resident of Delaware with the unusual name Morgan ap Morgan.
Sometime between 1726 and 1732, Morgan built a log house at the
present-day city of Bunker Hill. The pioneer Morgan family
influenced the region for years to come. Zackquill Morgan, the
son of Morgan ap Morgan, helped found Morgantown.

Groups of Germans who had previously lived in Pennsylvania
also came to the Eastern Panhandle. Those Germans, who were
called the Pennsylvania Dutch, established a wilderness
community that eventually grew into the city of Shepherdstown.
Another early settler in the Eastern Panhandle was Robert Harper,
who started a ferryboat business on the Potomac River in 1734.
The town that developed around the boat landing came to be
called Harpers Ferry.

Settlement was slower in the south, where pioneers had to
struggle over the rugged Allegheny Mountains. The earliest
known settlement on the trans-Allegheny frontier was made by
Jacob Marlin and Stephen Sewell in 1749. The town of Marlinton
was named after Marlin, and Big Sewell Mountain was named
after his companion. But were the two men really friends? They
shared a tiny cabin until they had an argument about religion.
When a surveying crew found them two years later, Marlin was
living alone in the cabin while Sewell resided in a nearby
hollowed-out tree. Still, they claimed to be pals as long as they did
not discuss the Bible.

As an apprentice surveyor in 1747, George Washington visited western Virginia for the first time.

A young George Washington visited western Virginia for the first time in 1747. At that time, the future president was an apprentice working with a surveying company commissioned by Lord Fairfax, the largest landowner in Virginia. Washington bathed in the mineral waters of Berkeley Springs, and he was astonished by the beauty of the land around him. He returned again and again.

The Indians regarded the settlers as invaders of their ancient hunting grounds. Clashes between whites and Indians broke out all along Virginia's western frontier. During an attack in 1755, a band of Shawnees captured pioneer Mary Ingles near the present-day Virginia-West Virginia border and took her to their camp on the Ohio River. Ingles managed to escape and then complete a wild journey across what is now the Mountain State to her home in Virginia. Her reports on the land between the Blue Ridge Mountains and the Ohio River were invaluable to future settlers.

A TROUBLED FRONTIER

By 1758, about ten thousand white settlers lived in what is now the state of West Virginia. Almost all the pioneers operated farms in the Eastern Panhandle region. Frontier communities in the trans-Allegheny region were few and scattered. The future state was commonly called western Virginia, but the colony of Pennsylvania also claimed some of its territory. The French and their Indian allies coveted the territory as well. With so many rivals for the land, western Virginia became a battleground.

The fighting on the frontier was part of a larger conflict called the French and Indian War, fought between England and France from 1754 to 1763. Because of the war, pioneers of western Virginia lived in terror. Communities on the frontier often consisted of a few cabins clustered around a fort. When the Indians or French attacked, the settlers dropped their farm implements and dashed to the fort's protective walls. Many of the wilderness forts became the hubs of modern cities. Fort Blair was the focal point for today's city of Point Pleasant. Fort Fincastle, later renamed Fort Henry, protected the village of Wheeling.

A turning point in the French and Indian War came in 1758 when British and American troops captured the French-held Fort Duquesne at present-day Pittsburgh, Pennsylvania. After the fall of Fort Duquesne, an uneasy peace settled on the frontier. More settlers then pushed into western Virginia. Traveling by raft down the rivers was the easiest way to penetrate the rugged western Virginia lands. Consequently, new communities developed along the streams. The town of Lewisburg grew near the Greenbrier

During the French and Indian War, Fort Fincastle, later renamed Fort Henry, protected the village of Wheeling.

River. Montgomery was the first large settlement to appear on the Kanawha River.

The pioneers came despite a 1763 proclamation issued by British King George III forbidding further settlement west of the Alleghenies. The king hoped that his order prohibiting westward expansion by the colonists would put an end to the conflicts between the colonists and the Indians. But the proclamation was generally ignored. Dutch and German settlers could not read the king's order. The Scotch-Irish, who were the boldest pioneers in North America, would recognize no law forbidding them to seek untamed land.

Many newcomers to western Virginia claimed "tomahawk rights" to farms. To establish such rights, a frontier family marked trees with axes, thereby setting the boundaries of a future farm. In years to come, courts frequently gave legal title to claims originally carved out by tomahawks and axes.

From its beginning, western Virginia developed a separate identity from the older, eastern part of the colony. Virginia was a land of well-established towns, large plantations, and slavery. West of the mountains spread a raw frontier where there were no real cities, few slaves, and almost no plantations. As early as 1756, plans were discussed to establish a separate fourteenth colony on the trans-Allegheny frontier. The proposal to form a trans-Allegheny colony was sent to the British king, but it never progressed beyond the talking stage.

Clashes with Indians remained a constant threat on the frontier. However, one Indian leader, a Mingo chief named Logan, made great efforts to live in peace with the whites. Despite Logan's appeals for friendship, a band of drunken settlers murdered his wife and children. The senseless slaughter sent Logan on the warpath. Shawnee chief Cornstalk also took up arms. The result was the bloody Lord Dunmore's War, named after the strong-willed royal governor of Virginia. The war ended when Captain Andrew Lewis's Virginia army defeated Cornstalk in the Battle of Point Pleasant, fought in 1774. Some historians call the Point Pleasant engagement of Lord Dunmore's War the first battle of the American Revolution, because they believe that the British encouraged Cornstalk to wage war on American settlements. The battle has greater significance, however. The treaties that were negotiated with the Indians after the Battle of Point Pleasant kept the peace on the frontier during the early years of the American Revolution.

REVOLUTION!

"No taxation without representation!" was the cry that echoed through the East and spurred the Americans of the thirteen colonies to revolt against England. But on the western Virginia frontier, the hated British taxes—such as that on tea—were of little

Lord Dunmore's War, which began because a band of settlers murdered the family of Mingo chief Logan (above), ended in the Battle of Point Pleasant (right).

concern. Few tax collectors could reach the isolated settlements beyond the Appalachians. Still, western Virginia pioneers fought valiantly for their country's independence.

Between 1777 and 1782, western Virginia was the scene of savage battles pitting frontier people against Indians armed with British guns and often led by British officers. For a generation after the war, people living in the Appalachian region spoke with horror about the fighting that raged in 1777 — "the bloody year of the three 7s."

No frontier fort in the American West saw more ferocious battles than did Fort Henry, at present-day Wheeling. Three times Fort Henry was besieged by Indian allies of the British. The courage shown by the fort's defenders became the stuff of frontier legends. In 1777, during the first attack, Colonel Ebenezer Zane

Revolutionary War reenactments such as this one remind West Virginians of the important role their ancestors played in the American victory over England.

commanded a force made up mainly of women and children. Women sharpshooters, assisted by gun loaders as young as ten, drove the Indians away from the fort's walls. In another battle in 1777, Major Samuel McCulloch escaped from a band of Indians by spurring his horse off a tall cliff into a shallow creek. Miraculously, both McCulloch and his horse survived. Heroes in later attacks included the black slave Daddy Smith, who single-handedly defended a key wall, and Betty Zane, a young woman who dashed through gunfire to fetch a supply of gunpowder.

The settlers of western Virginia played an important role in the American victory over England. They protected the nation's back door, allowing the bulk of American forces to challenge the British in the East. When the war finally ended in 1783, a new era dawned in western Virginia and in the infant United States.

Chapter 5
THE ROAD TO STATEHOOD

THE ROAD TO STATEHOOD

*The views [from Huntersville, West Virginia] are
magnificent, the valley so beautiful, the scenery
so peaceful. What a glorious world Almighty God
has given us. How thankless and ungrateful we are
and how we labor to mar His gifts.*
—Robert E. Lee, Civil War general

TAMING THE FRONTIER

On the American frontier, bloody clashes between settlers and
Indians continued after the Revolutionary War. Communities in
the West made heroes out of Indian fighters. One of the most
notorious of those was western Virginia's Lewis Wetzel.

Wetzel grew up in the wilderness south of present-day
Wheeling. When he was only fourteen, his log-cabin community
was raided by a band of Wyandot warriors. His parents were
killed, and he was taken captive. Wetzel escaped, but swore
eternal vengeance. He became a one-man war party, dedicated to
killing Indians. Extremely swift and agile, Wetzel was able to load
a clumsy flintlock rifle while running at full speed. The Indians
called him "Deathwind." But he was so driven by hatred that he
caused more trouble than he resolved. Wetzel killed friendly
Indians and triggered wars that could have been avoided.

Ann Bailey was a famous wilderness scout and an Indian
fighter. Her first husband was killed by Indians in the 1774 Battle

Daniel Boone (left) and Ann Bailey (above) were famous western Virginia trailblazers.

of Point Pleasant. After his death, Ann took up his work as a frontier trailblazer. Indians feared her deadly shooting eye. Stories were told of how she once rode 100 miles (161 kilometers) through a dense forest to bring gunpowder to a besieged fort. Known for her ferocious determination to complete a task, frontier people called her "Mad Ann" Bailey.

Certainly the most celebrated western Virginia frontiersman was Daniel Boone. Between 1788 and 1799, Boone lived in a two-room log cabin at Point Pleasant, and in the Charleston region. Boone became a lieutenant colonel in the Kanawha County militia in 1789. In that same year, he was elected to the Virginia legislature. Eventually, Boone moved farther west. He was a restless pioneer of Scotch-Irish stock who considered a region to be crowded if he could see his neighbor's chimney smoke.

Quilting parties were occasions for socializing on the western Virginia frontier.

Although many frontier people were callous about killing Indians, Boone always tried to avoid fighting them. He was a great admirer of Native American culture.

Like Daniel Boone, the pioneers of western Virginia lived in log cabins that were about the size of a two-car garage. The fireplace served as the cooking stove as well as the cabin's only source of heat. Corn was the frontier family's primary crop. In the forests, they hunted deer, bears, and wild turkeys. When the hunting was good, meat was almost as plentiful as bread. During the winter months, the people longed for spring "greenup time" when they could eat vegetables. One settler wrote, "I remember how narrowly the children watched the growth of the potato tops, pumpkins, and squash vines. . . . How delicious was the taste of young potatoes when we got them. What a jubilee when we were permitted to pull the young corn for roasting ears."

On the western Virginia frontier, disease was a far greater peril than were Indians. Measles, whooping cough, and diphtheria killed many children. With few doctors to consult, the pioneer people treated sicknesses with medicines made from tree bark, roots, and herbs. They learned some of these remedies, which proved to be remarkably effective, from the Indians. Virginia snakeroot was made into a syrup that controlled coughs. Often, the people relied on superstition to curb the ravages of illness. For example, many settlers believed that rheumatism could be cured if the sufferer turned his or her shoes upside down before going to bed.

Despite the hardships they endured, the people of western Virginia found endless ways to have fun. Children played hide-and-seek in the woods and London Bridge in the meadows. Boys held shooting matches and tomahawk-throwing contests. Women and girls gathered for quilting and apple-peeling parties. Weddings were popular and often riotous community events.

Sunday church meetings brought the far-flung frontier families together. A log-cabin church was usually the first community structure built by those pioneers. Early in the frontier era, however, church buildings did not exist, and "circuit-riding" ministers held meetings in cornfields and preached from their wagons. One of the most famous of those pioneer ministers was Francis Asbury, who preached the gospel in log-cabin settlements from Florida to Pennsylvania.

After the Revolutionary War, settlements continued to grow in western Virginia. The 1790 census counted more than fifty-five thousand settlers living in western Virginia. By 1800, that number had increased to almost seventy-nine thousand. Indian troubles gradually diminished, and new towns sprang up: Clarksburg and Morgantown in 1785; Charles Town in 1786; Middletown,

Because coal was an excellent fuel for western Virginia's Great Kanawha
Valley salt producers (above), the state's coal industry grew in importance.

Frankfort, and West Liberty in 1787. In 1788, Fort Lee was built
near the junction of the Kanawha and Elk rivers, and around it
grew a community that became Charleston.

While most people hailed the growth and progress of western
Virginia, some were incurable trailblazers and cursed the advance
of civilization. One dismayed pioneer was Adam O'Brien, who
lamented, "[We] lived quite happy [in western Virginia] before
the Revolution, for then there was no law, no courts, and no
sheriffs and [the people] agreed pretty well, but after awhile the
people began to come and made settlements and then there was
need for laws; and then came the lawyers . . . and from that time
we never had any peace any more."

EARLY INDUSTRY AND TRANSPORTATION

Salt was western Virginia's first major industry. Long before the
army of settlers came, the Delawares and other Indian groups took

salt from deposits along the Little Kanawha River. In the early 1800s, commercial salt mills opened in Bulltown and in Clarksburg. Salt production increased dramatically when two brothers, Joseph and David Ruffner, set up operations farther south in the Great Kanawha Valley. Soon, the Great Kanawha Valley was one of the world's great salt-producing regions.

Salt making spurred the growth of western Virginia's coal industry. Saltwater, called brine, that was taken from wells had to be boiled for hours to produce salt crystals. Wood burned too quickly to be a dependable source of heat for commercial salt kettles. So the salt makers tried coal and found it to be an excellent fuel. As early as 1742, John Peter Salley had discovered coal near the present-day village of Peytona. Probably no one involved in the pioneer salt and coal businesses guessed that coal would one day become the keystone industry for a new state.

Western Virginia's iron industry began in 1794 when Peter Tarr opened a large plant on King's Creek near present-day Weirton. At peak production, the plant turned out 2 tons (1.8 metric tons) of iron a day. Tarr's furnace produced the cannonballs used by naval commander Oliver Perry to blast British ships during the War of 1812.

During those same years, western Virginia witnessed many improvements in transportation. Newly developed steamboats churning down the Ohio River added excitement to life on the western Virginia frontier. At the cry, "Steamboat 'round the bend!" the residents of sleepy river towns ran to the wharves to watch the lumbering giants pass. One of the first commercially successful river steamboats was the *George Washington*, built at Wheeling in 1817.

The most important highway in the American West—the National Road, completed to Wheeling in 1818—cut through the

Northern Panhandle of present-day West Virginia. The National Road linked Cumberland, Maryland, with Wheeling in western Virginia, and eventually pushed west to the Mississippi River. Though it crossed only a tiny strip of the present state, the National Road helped make Wheeling a bustling trade center.

The Northwest Turnpike, an all-Virginia road, was completed in 1838. The western portion of the Northwest Turnpike ran through Romney, Grafton, Clarksburg, and Pennsboro, terminating at Parkersburg.

The new roads were used by farmers to drive cattle and haul goods to market. Stagecoach lines raced passengers over the roads at an average speed of 10 miles (16 kilometers) per hour. The ride was so jarring that passengers nicknamed the coaches "shakeguts."

Certainly a smoother way to transport people was by the railroads that were then being developed in the East. The Baltimore & Ohio Railroad (B&O) was the first major line to cross western Virginia. Work on the B&O began in 1827, but twenty-six years passed before the tracks reached Wheeling. The line's progress was delayed by jealous politicians who wanted the railroad to run through their towns, and by settlers fearful that the train would frighten their children and run over their livestock. Also, the task of building a railroad over western Virginia's endless rivers and through its many mountains was enormous. When completed, the B&O ran through 11 tunnels and over 113 bridges on its route from Cumberland to Wheeling.

VIRGINIA VERSUS WESTERN VIRGINIA

More and more, the western region of Virginia had established a vastly different character from the eastern region. Some of the differences stemmed from the land. The coastal plains of old Virginia supported large tobacco farms and cotton plantations. Agriculture in the west was limited to small farms tucked in river valleys. The people differed, too. Westerners tended to be of German or Scotch-Irish descent, while the easterners were mainly of English stock. Many political issues divided the west from the east. Virginia's government was dominated by wealthy plantation owners who often ignored the needs of small farmers west of the Alleghenies.

Trying to iron out the problems between east and west, Virginians held constitutional conventions in 1829 and again in 1850. Westerners wanted a fairer basis for representation in the state legislature. They also wanted all men, not just property owners, to have the right to vote. The first convention, however, was dominated by eastern plantation owners, and the westerners received no satisfaction. During the 1850 convention, the powerful plantation owners made some concessions. The basis for representation in the lower house of the legislature became more favorable to westerners, and all men were given the right to vote. Many delegates from western Virginia remained unhappy with the results.

A major split between east and west centered on the explosive issue of slavery. Aside from those on the large farms in the Eastern Panhandle, few slaves toiled in western Virginia. In contrast, slavery was a deeply entrenched institution on the plantations and tobacco farms of the east.

Western Virginia was home to a number of abolitionists—men and women who worked to end, or abolish, slavery. One opponent of slavery was Henry Ruffner, of the wealthy salt-merchant family. Ruffner favored laws that would give freedom to all slaves living in western Virginia. However, not all western

Virginians opposed slavery. Proslavery sentiment was strongest in the Eastern Panhandle, which held the region's largest slave population. It was in the Eastern Panhandle that the actions of an idealistic madman helped push the United States ever closer to civil war.

JOHN BROWN'S RAID ON HARPERS FERRY

John Brown was an unsuccessful businessman who had campaigned against slavery all his life. While living in Kansas, he and his followers brutally murdered five proslavery settlers. He dismissed the deaths as the Lord's will because he believed that God had commanded him to end the practice of slavery in the United States. Pursued by the law, Brown moved to a Maryland farm just 5 miles (8 kilometers) from the Eastern Panhandle town of Harpers Ferry. Several northerners supported his antislavery efforts and supplied him with money. Brown used the money to buy rifles, ammunition, and bayonets.

On October 16, 1859, Brown and eighteen other armed men took possession of Harpers Ferry. In the town stood a government arsenal where weapons were stored and a gun works where rifles were made. Details of his plans were vague, but Brown dreamed of giving the weapons to the slaves and leading them in rebellion.

Word of the invasion reached the Virginia militia stationed at Charles Town. Soon troops surrounded Harpers Ferry. After a day of wild gunfire, a company of marines led by Colonel Robert E. Lee—who later served as the commander for the Army of Northern Virginia during the Civil War—rushed the engine house where Brown and his men had taken refuge. In the fighting, several soldiers and civilians were killed. Brown was taken prisoner.

Abolitionist John Brown (above) and his followers were captured by a company of marines (left) after his raid on Harpers Ferry.

John Brown's raid on Harpers Ferry shocked and enraged southerners. Since Brown was supported by northern money, many southerners considered the seizure of the town to be a deliberate act of war. Brown was convicted of treason against the state of Virginia and was hanged on December 2, 1859. He found a measure of immortality, however, in the chorus of a popular marching song that was later sung by northern soldiers:

> John Brown's body lies a-mouldering in the grave,
> But his soul goes marching on.

A STATE BORN IN WAR

The cannon fire that rocked Fort Sumter, off South Carolina, on April 12, 1861, plunged the United States into the terrible Civil War. In terms of blood spilled, it was the costliest conflict in the nation's history. More Americans lost their lives in the Civil War than in World War II, the Korean War, and Vietnam combined.

It was during the turmoil of this dreadful war that West Virginia became a state. Only five days after the bombardment of Fort Sumter, a convention met at the city of Richmond and declared that the state of Virginia would secede from the American Union. However, the overwhelming majority of convention delegates from Virginia's western regions voted against secession. One of those delegates was John S. Carlile, a lawyer who lived in Clarksburg. Carlile and other westerners organized two conventions that met in Wheeling. The second convention declared that western Virginia would form a separate state. A general election held on October 24, 1861, confirmed the will of the Wheeling convention. By a huge majority of 18,408 to 781, the voters of western Virginia favored the formation of a separate state.

Wheeling served as the capital of the newly formed state. Naming the state was one of the first orders of business. Various names were considered, including Kanawha, Allegheny, and Augusta. Finally, political leaders agreed on the name West Virginia.

After a lengthy debate, the United States Congress approved a bill allowing West Virginia to enter the Union. President Abraham Lincoln signed the bill, and on June 20, 1863, West Virginia became the nation's thirty-fifth state. Arthur I. Boreman was West Virginia's first governor.

During the Civil War, few large land battles were fought on West Virginia's soil. Most of the time the state was securely in the hands of Union forces. But West Virginia was raided often by southern troops seeking to interrupt the B&O Railroad, or to secure salt, which was scarce in the South. More than thirty thousand West Virginia men served in the Union ranks. Prosouthern sentiment remained strong in some parts of the state, however, and some seven thousand West Virginians fought on the Confederate side.

The famous family feud between the Hatfields and the McCoys began during the Civil War. The Hatfields, from West Virginia, sided with the Confederates. The McCoys, most of whom lived across the border in Kentucky, enlisted in the Union army. A shooting war broke out between the two clans when a pig ran away from one family's farm and was claimed by the other family. Fighting between the clans lasted for several generations and resulted in at least a dozen killings.

EARLY STATE POLITICS

When the Civil War ended, the state of Virginia asked West Virginia to reunite with it and form one state as had been the case in the past. West Virginia soundly rejected the offer. In a letter written in 1866, the West Virginia state legislature said, "The people of this state are unalterably opposed to reunion . . . and will not entertain any proposition looking to that end." With no hope of regaining her old western region, Virginia presented West Virginia with a shocking bill. Virginia claimed that West Virginia owed millions of dollars as its share of the state debt incurred before the Civil War. The question of state debt went to court and bounced about the legal system for forty-five years before it was settled, with West Virginia eventually paying $12.4 million.

Bitterness over Civil War loyalties lingered in West Virginia long after the end of hostilities. At the urging of former Union soldiers, the state legislature passed a law denying the vote to all West Virginians who had fought for the Confederacy. Outrage over the law led to heated arguments as well as fistfights on town streets. Finally, in 1871, state senator W. H. H. Flick, himself a

Union veteran, led a movement to restore voting privileges to all former Confederate soldiers. The revised law allowed Henry Mason Mathews, who had fought for the South, to run for governor. Mathews was elected in 1876, and became one of the finest governors in the early history of the state.

A special election was held in 1877, permitting the people to select a town to be their permanent state capital. Among the choices for a new capital city were Clarksburg, Martinsburg, and Charleston. The people chose Charleston, and the state capital was officially moved there in 1885.

ECONOMIC DEVELOPMENTS

Railroads led the industrial expansion that swept West Virginia after the Civil War. The most important new railroad was the Chesapeake and Ohio, which was completed in 1873 and linked the Atlantic Ocean city of Norfolk, Virginia, to the Ohio River town of Huntington, West Virginia. Collis P. Huntington, a California millionaire who helped build the first transcontinental railroad, financed the Chesapeake and Ohio. The city of Huntington is named after this bold railroad pioneer. The Chesapeake and Ohio spurred the growth of many towns along its route, including Ronceverte, Hinton, Montgomery, and St. Albans.

New railroads hauled West Virginia's coal to faraway markets. In turn, the railroads were one of the coal industry's biggest customers because the steam-driven engines had an enormous appetite for the black fuel. Many of the state's industrial leaders invested their money in both coal and railroads.

Two of West Virginia's richest industrialists were Henry Gassaway Davis and his son-in-law Stephen Elkins. Davis was born into poverty and began his career as a brakeman on freight

Railroad builders Henry G. Davis (left) and his son-in-law Stephen Elkins became two of West Virginia's richest industrialists.

trains. At the age of eighty, he financed the building of the Potomac and Piedmont Railroad, which served coal towns in the central part of the state. Stephen Elkins, for whom the town of Elkins is named, was also a railroad builder. Both men had a passionate interest in politics and served West Virginia in the United States Senate. Elkins served as secretary of war under President Benjamin Harrison. Davis, who was called "West Virginia's Grand Old Man," was the Democratic party's nominee for vice-president of the United States in 1904.

By the early 1900s, oil and natural gas enjoyed increased production in West Virginia. As early as 1860, a primitive oil well that operated near the town of Burning Springs produced seven barrels of oil a day. In 1900, the state's oil production topped 16 million barrels. Natural gas had also been discovered in the state. By 1906, West Virginia led the nation in the output of natural gas.

Despite the impressive industrial expansion, West Virginia was an impoverished state at the turn of the century. Workers were underpaid, the school system was poorly funded, and roads were in disrepair. As West Virginia faced the new century, great strides were needed to make it a modern state.

Chapter 6
GROWTH
OF A
MODERN
STATE

GROWTH OF A MODERN STATE

*When the labor train rattles up the creek
in the foggy hour before dawn, and hundreds of
blurred shapes pile out . . . and the miners seek
their various mines—that is something which, seen
once, is never to be forgotten. And when, at the
end of the day, they all pile aboard the same train
and . . . bump down to a bleary mining camp—that
is something not to be forgotten either.*
—James M. Cain, 1924

KING COAL

Coal quickly became the leading industry of the Mountain State. In 1870, West Virginia's mines produced 600,000 tons (544,311 metric tons) of coal. Ten years later, that figure more than doubled. By 1900, the state had an annual coal yield of more than 21 million tons (19 million metric tons).

The coal industry brought a small army of miners and their families to West Virginia. Many mining families came from southern or eastern Europe. The European miners, arriving in the late 1800s and early 1900s, were the last great wave of foreigners to migrate to West Virginia. Finding housing was the first problem the newcomers faced. Since coal was often discovered far from population centers, mining companies built housing for their employees near the entrances of the mines. Many of those "company towns" rose in the southern half of the state.

Mining profits gave rise to a wealthy class of men who were called "coal barons." The McKell family were coal barons who ran a mining operation headquartered in the town of Glen Jean. Isaac T. Mann, another coal baron, lived in Bramwell, in southern West Virginia. Many of the coal barons held powerful positions in state government. Aretas Brooks Fleming was a mine owner who served as West Virginia's governor from 1890 to 1893. Another coal baron, Clarence Watson, was West Virginia's United States senator in the early 1900s.

LIFE IN THE MINING COMMUNITIES

For miners and their families, King Coal was a cruel monarch. Wages in the coal industry were low. Workers toiled long hours in pitch-dark, cramped mine shafts. Floors in the mine shafts were often knee-deep with water. Most miners were paid by the amount of coal they blasted out of the shaft and shoveled onto hopper cars. One miner remembered, "We worked for fifteen cents a ton. If we made a dollar and a half a day, we made pretty good money. You got up between three and four in the morning. We usually got out [of the mine shaft] around dark. Sometimes I didn't get home until ten at night. Those nights I was so tired I just laid back to sleep, didn't even wash up."

Nearly all aspects of life in a company town were dictated by the mine owner. A greedy mine owner was free to charge exorbitant rents, forcing mine-working families to reach into their food and clothing budgets. Since company towns were often tucked away in the hills far away from other communities, most families were forced to shop at the company store, where the mine owner determined the prices. Some mining companies refused to pay their workers in United States currency. Instead, the miners

Among the terrifying realities of coal-mining life in West Virginia are cave-ins and other deadly accidents. A 1907 mine explosion at the Monongah Mine, near Fairmont (above), killed 361 miners.

were issued paper scrip or copper tokens that were good only for buying supplies at the company store, thereby increasing the workers' dependence on the mine owner.

Company towns were patrolled by mine guards who were on duty to protect mine property. Often, however, the guards followed secret instructions and sought out what they called "union troublemakers." Townspeople suspected of being sympathetic to labor unions were beaten up or put in jail on trumped-up charges. In 1907, West Virginia governor William Dawson complained, "They [the guards] are used . . . to prevent labor agitators and organizers of miners' unions from gaining access to the miners. . . . Many outrages have been committed by these guards, many of whom appear to be vicious and daredevil men who seem to add to their viciousness by bulldozing and terrorizing people."

Not only were working conditions harsh, but coal mining was perhaps the most dangerous job in the United States. Coal in Appalachia is found in narrow seams that run through the mountains like icing in the middle of a layer cake. To extract the coal, workers burrowed a shaft into the seam. The ceiling of the mine shaft was held up by timbers. Mine cave-ins and other deadly accidents were—and continue to be—a terrifying reality of coal-mining life in West Virginia. An explosion at the Monongah Mine in 1907 killed 361 miners. In 1914, an explosion in a mine near Eccles cost 188 lives. In 1924, a mine accident killed 119 miners at Benwood.

THE LABOR WARS

Labor unions developed despite the efforts of mine owners to discourage union activity. Strikes in the railroad, steel, and coal industries rocked West Virginia in the late 1800s and early 1900s. Two strikes by coal miners—one beginning in 1912 and the other beginning in 1919—stand out as the bitterest and bloodiest in the state's history.

In 1912, miners along Paint Creek in Kanawha County walked off their jobs and declared a strike. They were quickly joined by members of the United Mine Workers of America (UMWA) who lived on Cabin Creek. The workers demanded a nine-hour day, improved housing in company towns, and payment in United States currency rather than paper scrip or copper coins that were good only at the company store. The mine owners retaliated by evicting the striking workers and their families. Thrown out of their homes, the men, women, and children set up tent cities on the outskirts of the company towns. The strike dragged on for months.

Aiding the striking miners was the remarkable Mary Harris "Mother" Jones. Born in Ireland, Mother Jones became a UMWA organizer at age sixty-one. She lived to be one hundred years old and remained devoted to the labor movement. Tough as the grittiest miner, she counseled families and gave heart to discouraged strikers. Above all, she cautioned striking workers to shun violence because any destruction of mine property or loss of life would bring the weight of the law down on the union.

The uneasy peace at Paint Creek was shattered when a band of men raked a tent community with rifle fire. One striking miner was killed and many were injured in the hail of bullets. The outraged miners took up hunting rifles and marched on the town of Mucklow, present-day Gallagher. A pitched battle between miners and mine guards left a dozen workers and four guards dead. Governor William Glasscock declared martial law and sent the state militia to the Paint Creek region. More than a hundred union members, including Mother Jones, were arrested. A new governor, Henry Hatfield, took office in 1913, and released most of the strikers from jail. Hatfield also persuaded the mine owners to raise pay and improve conditions in the mines.

In 1917, the demands of the United States' involvement in World War I drove up the price of coal and brought a period of prosperity to the state. But coal prices dropped after the war, and another bloody strike swept Logan and Mingo counties.

At first, violence in southern West Virginia was averted by a daring act of Governor John Cornwell. At the town of Marmet, Cornwell spoke to a group of several hundred angry miners, many of whom were armed with rifles. The miners had gathered at Marmet with the intention of marching south to show support

When a battle broke out in 1912 between striking mine workers and mine guards near Paint Creek, Governor William Glasscock (right) declared martial law and arrested more than a hundred union members, including union organizer Mary Harris "Mother" Jones (left).

for the UMWA workers on strike. Delivering an impassioned speech, Cornwell implored the miners to give up their march, as it could lead to a violent conflict with mine guards. The vast majority of miners heeded the governor's words and returned home. Then, in May of 1920, a shooting spree exploded between miners and mine guards at the town of Matewan. Three months later, workers and guards clashed again. At least fifteen people were killed and dozens were injured in the two battles. Around the nation, newspapers called Mingo County "Bloody Mingo."

The labor war broke out again in 1921 when UMWA members marched on the city of Logan. They were met at the nearby village of Blair by mine owners who had assembled a small army of guards equipped with machine guns. The mine owners even rented combat airplanes in their determination to stop the march.

During the Great Depression, the Civilian Conservation Corps set up camps throughout the state to house the workers who would build roads and highways, cut hiking trails, or build fire-watch stations. These young men lived at Camp Marshall, near Moundsville.

A four-day battle ensued. Governor Cornwell asked President Warren Harding to send in units of the United States Army, as the state militia was clearly unable to stop the bloodshed. A detachment of two thousand troops and a squadron of fighter aircraft finally brought some semblance of peace to southern West Virginia.

The labor war at Logan and Mingo counties ended as a victory for the mine owners. The companies ignored the union's demands and the demoralized workers gradually went back to their jobs. Because of the defeat, union membership suffered. In 1920, the UMWA had forty-five thousand members in West Virginia; nine years later, their rolls had dropped to about one thousand.

DEPRESSION AND WORLD WAR II RECOVERY

The Great Depression of the 1930s shut down industry in the United States and throughout much of the world. Nationally, one

Eleanor Roosevelt, wife of President Franklin D. Roosevelt, helped supervise the building of housing at Arthurdale for families from abandoned coal-mining towns and logging camps.

in four workers lost their jobs. In West Virginia, the unemployment rate was even higher.

With aid from the federal government under President Franklin Roosevelt's New Deal, several projects were launched with the goal of putting jobless Mountaineers on a payroll. The Civilian Conservation Corps (CCC) gave unemployed young men work in the forests, cutting hiking trails and building fire-watch stations. The CCC spent $7.5 million in West Virginia and set up fifty-two camps throughout the state to house the young workers. The Federal Emergency Relief Administration (FERA) employed sixty thousand West Virginians to build roads and highways. Altogether, the FERA spent $51 million in West Virginia.

A frequent visitor to the state during the depression was Eleanor Roosevelt, wife of the president. Mrs. Roosevelt acted as an administrator for several depression-relief programs. In West

Virginia, she helped supervise the building of government housing near the town of Arthurdale. The new houses were used to resettle families from abandoned coal-mining towns and logging camps. To show their appreciation, the people of West Virginia named a town Eleanor in honor of the First Lady.

The Japanese bombs that rained down at Pearl Harbor on December 7, 1941, snapped the nation out of the Great Depression. With the country's entry into World War II, the price of coal rose and there was ample work in the mines. The steel mills at Wheeling and Weirton hummed with activity. Boat yards at Point Pleasant turned out landing craft and other small ships. The world's largest synthetic rubber plant was built at Institute. One factory in South Charleston produced more than 131,000 gun barrels for the United States Navy.

But, as always, wartime prosperity came with a terrible price tag. Almost 250,000 Mountaineers served in the armed forces during the war years, and 5,830 lost their lives in the conflict.

THE POSTWAR ERA

Most regions of the United States enjoyed a period of prosperity during the 1950s, but West Virginia's economy underwent a time of painful adjustment. Once more, the coal industry was crucial to the state's prospects. People working in the coal industry suffered two setbacks. First, the use of coal declined as industries and households switched to other sources of fuel. Second, automated machinery introduced into the mines produced rivers of coal with the help of very few laborers.

Steel making and glassmaking expanded in the postwar period, but those industries were unable to absorb all the workers made jobless by developments in the coal industry. In the years after

'Real Gold in Them Thar Hills!'

Roman Catholic Senator John F. Kennedy's primary election victory in overwhelmingly Protestant West Virginia was an important milestone on his road to the presidency.

World War II, the great West Virginia exodus began. With little prospect of finding work, thousands of West Virginians left their home state to seek employment in industrial cities in the North. The people who fled tended to be the youngest and brightest, while those who remained were often the elderly who collected some sort of public aid. In the decade of the 1950s, the exodus reduced West Virginia's population by 7 percent.

The Mountain State received an important visitor in 1960 when Massachusetts Senator John F. Kennedy campaigned there. Kennedy hoped to become the first Roman Catholic to be elected president of the United States. By starting his long road to the White House in overwhelmingly Protestant West Virginia, he took a bold gamble. Many important politicians within Kennedy's own Democratic party believed that Mountaineers were too bigoted to vote for a Catholic. The eyes of the nation were fixed on

This Union Carbide plant near Charleston, along with other large chemical plants in the state, now provides jobs for many West Virginians.

West Virginia on May 10, 1960, the day of the Democratic primary election. The results were surprising. The American people learned that West Virginians harbored little religious bias, as Kennedy defeated his rival, Hubert Humphrey, by a margin of almost 100,000 votes.

As president, Kennedy repaid the people of West Virginia by backing a measure designed to help all the depressed states of the Appalachian region. Under Kennedy, and later under President Lyndon Johnson, federal programs provided funds to restore forests, build roads, and retrain workers who had lost their coal-mining jobs. Despite the measure, the exodus of job-seeking Mountaineers continued. Between 1960 and 1970, the Mountain State lost 6 percent of its population.

Two disasters shook West Virginia late in the postwar era. The first tragedy was sadly familiar. In 1968, a coal mine at Farmington exploded, killing 78 miners. The explosion spurred the United States Congress to make new laws tightening safety regulations in the mines. Congress also voted to give disability funds to miners and former miners suffering from pneumoconiosis, a deadly illness also known as "black lung disease." Many mine workers developed black lung disease after decades of breathing coal dust. The second disaster struck near the town of Man in 1972. After heavy rainfall had swelled Buffalo Creek, a dam—poorly constructed from mine refuse—suddenly collapsed. The resulting onrush of water killed 125 people, making it the worst flood in the state's history.

WEST VIRGINIA TODAY

New industries have risen to replace the state's reliance on coal. Great salt deposits discovered along the Ohio River serve as the basis of the state's chemical industry. Chemical plants convert salt into products such as bromide, which is added to gasoline to make car engines run smoothly. During the 1970s, the chemical industry provided jobs for twenty-seven thousand West Virginians. Today, large chemical plants stand at Belle, Charleston, South Charleston, Institute, and Parkersburg.

Also in the 1970s, the glassmaking industry employed as many as fourteen thousand Mountaineers. The state has an ample supply of silica, a material used in the glassmaking process. In addition, West Virginia's large reserves of natural gas are essential to heat glassmaking ovens. Major glass factories are at Huntington, Weston, Williamstown, Morgantown, New Martinsville, Moundsville, and Milton.

Although rival industries have grown in the state, coal remains its economic lifeblood. Consequently, West Virginia continues to be locked into the boom-or-bust coal cycle. The price of coal jumped in the early 1970s when suppliers from the Middle East reduced the amount of oil they shipped to the United States. The higher prices spurred coal production and generated jobs in the mines. But the West Virginia economy slowed down again during the general business slump of the early 1980s. Through much of the decade of the 1980s, West Virginia had the nation's worst unemployment rate. Also, the exodus picked up once more, and the state lost population between 1980 and 1990.

Two political leaders dominated the governor's office in the modern era. Arch Moore, a veteran Republican, first won the governorship in 1968. After serving two terms, Moore was replaced by Democrat John D. (Jay) Rockefeller IV, scion of the wealthy New York family. Rockefeller had come to West Virginia in the 1960s as a young antipoverty worker.

For many years, the issue of strip mining divided Moore and Rockefeller. Strip mining is a method of extracting coal by digging up whole mountaintops rather than by tunneling. Although strip mining is a safer, more efficient way to take out coal, it leaves ugly gouges in the earth. Initially, Rockefeller opposed strip mining while Moore favored it. Rockefeller was elected governor only after he softened his position against strip mining. During his term in office, however, West Virginia's laws on strip mining came closer to federal regulations. In 1984, West Virginians once again elected Moore to the governorship and elected Rockefeller to the United States Senate. Both men have used their positions to encourage new industries in the state.

Gaston Caperton, a Democrat, defeated Arch Moore in his 1988 bid for reelection as governor. Once in office, Caperton proposed

Today, tourism is one of the greatest growth industries in West Virginia. This stern-wheeler transports visitors to and from Blennerhassett Island.

far-reaching reforms. To help pay West Virginia's debts, the sales tax on gasoline and groceries was increased. Teachers now earn higher salaries, and more schools are being built. West Virginia's government continues to encourage new industries and businesses.

Today, tourism is one of the greatest growth industries in modern West Virginia. More than forty thousand Mountaineers hold jobs in tourist-related companies. Economists cite the state's improved roads, which have encouraged millions of visitors to come to West Virginia each year. But certainly the state's unspoiled beauty also lures tourists. The forested mountains, the vast state park system, and the welcoming smiles of friendly residents will keep the tourists coming to the Mountain State in the future.

Chapter 7
GOVERNMENT AND THE ECONOMY

GOVERNMENT AND THE ECONOMY

The capitol building at Charleston is the seat of state government. The sprawling steel mills at Weirton are an example of private enterprise in action. Cooperation between the state government and private enterprise is essential to the well-being of modern West Virginia.

STATE GOVERNMENT

West Virginia is governed by its second constitution, which was written in 1872 and amended, or changed, more than fifty times. Amendments can be made at special constitutional conventions or can be added to the constitution if approved by more than two-thirds of the state legislature and a majority of the voters.

A constitution provides rules for running a government. West Virginia's constitution divides the state government into three departments: executive, legislative, and judicial.

The executive department is responsible for carrying out the state's laws. It is headed by the governor, who is elected to a four-year term. The constitution prohibits the governor from serving more than two consecutive terms. As chief executive, the governor is permitted to call out the National Guard in cases of emergency. The governor also chooses the department heads of many powerful state agencies. Other important officers in the executive department include the secretary of state, the auditor, and the attorney general. All these officers are elected to four-year terms.

The legislative department creates new laws and rescinds old laws. The West Virginia legislature consists of two houses: the senate and the house of delegates. The senate has thirty-four members and the house of delegates one hundred members. Senators are elected to four-year terms, while members of the house serve two-year terms. Men and women of the legislature debate proposed laws, called bills. When both houses agree on the wording of a bill, it is sent to the governor's office. The bill becomes a law when it is signed by the governor.

The judicial department is made up of the state court system. West Virginia's highest court is the supreme court of appeals, which has five judges, all of whom are elected to twelve-year terms. Below the supreme court are circuit courts and magistrate courts. Each West Virginia county has at least one magistrate court. The court system is called upon to listen to cases as grave as murder or as routine as a minor traffic offense.

Money is the most hotly debated subject in state government. Annual budgets exceed $1.75 billion. Revenue comes from a sales tax, a personal income tax, a corporate tax, and levies on such items as gasoline and alcohol. In 1985, West Virginia established a state lottery to produce more income.

Local governments are administered by the state's fifty-five counties and many municipalities. Maintaining parks and providing a town police force are among the functions of local government.

EDUCATION

Maintaining the public school system is the most expensive single item in the state budget. It costs about $3,000 per year to educate each West Virginia student. State law requires that all

West Virginia University at Morgantown (above) is the state's largest institute of higher learning. The University of Charleston (left) is one of West Virginia's many privately supported colleges.

children from ages seven through fifteen attend school. The state has about 358,000 elementary and secondary school students. Some 12,000 West Virginia students attend private schools. Most West Virginia private schools are church-affiliated.

West Virginia has nineteen accredited universities and colleges. The state's oldest college is Bethany, founded in 1840. Serving more than 19,000 students, the state-supported West Virginia University in Morgantown is the largest institute of higher learning. Other state-supported schools include Concord College, in Athens; Marshall University, in Huntington; Shepherd College, in Shepherdstown; and West Virginia State College, in Institute. Among the many privately supported colleges are the University of Charleston, in Charleston; Wheeling Jesuit College, in Wheeling; Davis and Elkins College, in Elkins; West Virginia Wesleyan College, in Buckhannon; and Alderson-Broaddus College, in Philippi.

The Mountain State was home to Booker T. Washington, one of the most influential educators in American history. Born to a slave family in 1856, Booker T. Washington grew up in the town of Malden. As a youth, he worked in salt furnaces and coal mines.

Though the state's mountains are a detriment to large-scale farming, many small farms prosper.

Although he was desperately poor, Washington had a hunger to learn and eventually earned a college degree. Washington later moved to Alabama, where he was one of the founders of Tuskegee Institute, a college serving black youths. He also served as an advisor to members of Congress and to various presidents.

AGRICULTURE

West Virginia's many mountains are a detriment to farming. In the 1980s, West Virginia ranked only forty-sixth among the fifty states in farm production. The state's farms tend to be small, averaging some 172 acres (70 hectares) in size.

Dairy farms once prevailed in the state, but by the 1980s livestock breeding had become the leading farm enterprise. Hay, most of which is fed to cattle, is the state's most valuable field crop. Corn and tobacco are other important crops. Apples and peaches are grown in Eastern Panhandle orchards. West Virginia farmers were the first in the nation to produce Golden Delicious apples. Poultry farmers in Hardy County raise about 10 million chickens each year.

MINING AND NATURAL RESOURCES

What West Virginia lacks in farmland it makes up in natural resources. The state has almost 12 million acres (5 million hectares) of commercial forestland. It ranks among the leading states in harvesting hardwoods such as cherry, oak, and tulip trees. Vast salt deposits lie under the Ohio and Kanawha river valleys. Petroleum and natural gas fields are located in the Appalachian Plateau. Limestone is taken from mines in the eastern mountains. Sand and gravel are also produced in West Virginia.

West Virginia is the nation's third-leading coal producer, ranking behind Kentucky and Wyoming. The type of coal found in southern West Virginia is especially valuable because it gives off very little pollution when it is burned. Even though coal has been mined commercially in West Virginia for more than one hundred years, vast fields of the black fuel remain. Engineers estimate that only 15 percent of the state's coal reserve has been mined.

MANUFACTURING

Factories in West Virginia produce about $4 billion worth of products each year. The chemical industry is the state's largest manufacturing enterprise. West Virginia chemical plants turn out dyes, detergents, oil additives, synthetic rubber, paints, and plastics. The state's steel industry is centered in the Northern Panhandle cities of Wheeling and Weirton. Mills in Wheeling produce huge steel I beams used in construction.

West Virginia is famous for producing fine glass items. Delicate glass dinnerware that graces the nation's tables is made in

Chester, Clarksburg, Morgantown, Newell, Salem, Weston, and Williamstown. Bottles, plate glass, and glass brick are made at plants throughout the state.

SERVICE INDUSTRIES

More than half the jobs open to West Virginians are in service industries. About 22 percent of the state's workers are employed in wholesale or retail trade, a leading service industry. The government employs another 21 percent. Banking, insurance, and real estate are other important service industries.

Each year, millions of tourists come to West Virginia. Restaurant workers, hotel clerks, guides, park workers, and others who attend to the needs of the tourists are service workers. They provide a service instead of manufacturing products. The tourist industry is important to large cities and small towns alike.

TRANSPORTATION AND COMMUNICATION

West Virginia has about 4,000 miles (6,437 kilometers) of railroad track and 35,000 miles (56,326 kilometers) of roads. Railroads still haul millions of tons of coal, but passenger service has declined sharply. The West Virginia Turnpike, which runs through the heart of the state, was completed in 1955 and is hailed as a marvel of engineering. Improved roads throughout the state have led to a dramatic increase in tourism.

River transport has always been vital to mountainous West Virginia. Today the state has about 500 miles (805 kilometers) of navigable waterways. The Ohio River is the state's economic lifeline, carrying barges loaded with coal, lumber, oil, chemicals, and steel to the Mississippi River before their trip to the Gulf of

Tourism—an industry important to the state's cities, towns, and resorts—provides jobs for many West Virginians.

Mexico. Today, more West Virginia coal is carried by river barges than by trains.

West Virginia also has about forty-five airports. Charleston is the center of the state's air traffic.

The Mountain State has seventy-five newspapers, including twenty-five dailies. The first newspaper in the state was printed in Shepherdstown in 1790. Among the largest daily newspapers are the *Charleston Gazette*, the *Huntington Herald-Dispatch*, the *Parkersburg News*, and the *Wheeling News-Register*. The state also has twelve television stations and one hundred radio stations.

Chapter 8

ARTS AND ENTERTAINMENT

ARTS AND ENTERTAINMENT

Throughout its history, West Virginia has nurtured art, literature, sports, and leisure-time activities. The talents displayed by its citizens have greatly enhanced the quality of life in the Mountain State.

ARTS AND CRAFTS

Though their names have been forgotten to history, the quilt makers of the West Virginia frontier produced fine works of art. Quilt making was a group activity. At a "quilting bee," women got together to stitch and chat. Many of the quilts they worked on were given to brides as wedding presents. Especially decorative quilts were given romantic names such as "Sunrise on the Wall of Troy," "Wonder of the Forest," "Noah's Dove," and "Maid of Orleans." Some of the quilts made by the skilled hands of pioneer women hang in art museums. Quilts made by today's West Virginia quilters are sought after by tourists.

In the early twentieth century, glassmakers and potters brought West Virginia handicrafts to other states. The Blenko glass company in Milton specialized in producing fine stained glass for churches and other buildings. Only talented glassmakers who had trained for years could produce this material correctly. Glass from the Blenko company went into many famous buildings, including the Washington National Cathedral in Washington, D.C., and the

Quilts and pottery made by today's West Virginia artists and craftspeople are sought after by tourists.

Cathedral of St. John the Divine in New York City. The town of Blacksville was a pottery center where master potters gathered to produce vases and other items from local clay.

One of the state's first notable artists was Elliot Daingerfield, who was born at Harpers Ferry in 1859 but moved to North Carolina at an early age. Daingerfield's landscape and figure paintings were hailed in America and Europe. Another gifted early artist was Joseph H. Diss Debar, who lived in Doddridge County during the post-Civil War years. Among his other accomplishments, Debar designed the state seal and coat of arms, which are still in use. Debar also published the first *Handbook of West Virginia*, a book that contained many of his illustrations.

Contemporary artists enjoy an enthusiastic following in West Virginia. The late Blanche Lazzell, of Morgantown, is famed for her murals (wall paintings) and for her color wood-block prints. Grace Martin Taylor, of Charleston, is a noted modern painter and an art teacher. William Hopen, who works out of a studio in Sutton, is a modern sculptor who creates large bronze pieces.

LITERATURE

West Virginia's first accomplished novelist was Rebecca Harding Davis, who lived in Wheeling during the Civil War era. Davis wrote about the struggles of working people and small farmers. Her short story "Life in the Iron Mills" told of a mill hand who strove to break the grip of poverty. In the novel *David Gaunt*, Davis dramatized the life of a family trying to eke out a living on a small West Virginia farm.

Years after the Civil War freed his family, educator Booker T. Washington, who grew up in West Virginia, published his autobiography, *Up From Slavery*. Washington believed that former slaves would prosper in America if they were given job training and a proper education. His book, which was widely read throughout the United States, explained his theories.

In the late 1800s and early 1900s, West Virginia short-story writers won national fame. One was Frank R. Stockton, who lived in Jefferson County and published a popular story called "The Lady or the Tiger?" Stockton's story ends as a man is given a choice of opening one of two doors: behind one is a beautiful woman; behind the other is a man-eating tiger. Melville Davisson Post, who was born near Clarksburg, wrote popular detective stories. One of the characters Post created was Uncle Abner, a wealthy farmer who became an amateur detective. Margaret Prescott Montague, of White Sulphur Springs, won the 1920 O. Henry Memorial Prize for her story "England to America," a work that urged greater cooperation between the two nations.

Probably the finest writer native to the Mountain State was Pearl S. Buck, born in Hillsboro in 1892. At a very young age, Buck moved to China with her missionary parents. Most of her novels are set in that country. She won the 1932 Pulitzer Prize in

Pearl Buck (above), who was born in this house in Hillsboro (left), is probably the finest writer native to West Virginia.

fiction for *The Good Earth*. Buck is the only woman writer to win both the Pulitzer Prize and the Nobel Prize in literature, which she won in 1938.

Jean Lee Latham, of Buckhannon, is a writer of books for young readers. Some of her titles are *The Story of Eli Whitney, Medals for Morse*, and *Trail Blazers of the Sea*. Latham's historical novel *Carry On, Mr. Bowditch* won the Newbery Medal as the best young person's book of 1956.

Mary Lee Settle is a contemporary writer who uses West Virginia as the setting for many of her books. Her 1989 novel *Charley Bland* concerns a young woman who is lured away from West Virginia by an exciting job in New York City. The woman then returns home to face a complicated period of readjustment in her native state.

THE DRAMATIC ARTS

Amateur and professional theater groups are active in nearly all parts of West Virginia. The Kanawha Players, a company based in

Charleston, is the state's oldest theater group. The Brooke Hills Playhouse Company, in Follansbee, performs in a remodeled, century-old barn. Lewisburg's historic Carnegie Hall is the stage for the Greenbrier Players.

The state sponsors an exciting summer theater program at five outdoor amphitheaters. The largest of these is the Cliffside Amphitheater, at Grandview State Park near Beckley. Two plays, both about West Virginia, are favorites at Cliffside. One play is *Honey in the Rock*, which dramatizes West Virginia's separation from Virginia during the Civil War. Another play staged during the summer season is *The Hatfields and the McCoys*, which tells about the famous feud between the two families. Well-known folksinger Billy Edd Wheeler spent much time researching the feud before writing this play.

Many West Virginians have contributed to television and the movies. During the 1930s, West Virginia-born Pare Lorentz produced award-winning documentary films about Americans confronted with the industrial age. Don Knotts, a comedian who has appeared on many television shows, was born in the Mountain State and is a graduate of West Virginia University. Actress Joanne Dru, who played opposite John Wayne in classic westerns such as *Red River* and *She Wore a Yellow Ribbon*, was born in Logan. Television journalist Tony Brown was raised in Charleston.

MUSIC

The Appalachian region has one of the richest musical traditions in the United States. Playing on buckskin banjos and homemade fiddles, the settlers of Appalachia created a unique form of folk music. Words to the folk songs were passed from

Folk music, one of the state's richest musical traditions, has its roots in the pioneer past.

farm to farm and from one frontier community to another. In many respects, the bluegrass music so loved in Appalachia today has roots in the region's pioneer past.

One of the most famous ballads associated with West Virginia is the work song "John Henry." Popular versions of this song portray folk hero John Henry as a muscular black railroad laborer who hammered steel rods into mountainsides as the first step in building the Big Bend Tunnel. In words and music, the song tells

West Virginia folk festivals feature traditional music, crafts, and culture.

of a fateful day when a man with a newly invented steam drill claimed that his machine could outwork any man. John Henry agreed to race the steam drill and thus set up a classic contest between man and machine. John Henry won the race, but he had worked himself into a state of exhaustion and collapsed and died. In a tragic last refrain, the song ends with the lines:

> He laid down his hammer and he died, Lawd, Lawd.
> Yes, he laid down his hammer and he died.

The Mountaineers' love for music in all its varieties is seen in the state's many public performances and music festivals. Bluegrass music is featured at the King Coal Festival held every year at Williamson. An even bigger event is the Summersville Music Park Bluegrass Country Music Festival, held each June. Lovers of pure folk music flock to the West Virginia State Folk Festival, held in Glenview, to hear artists render songs in the same manner as did the pioneers of Appalachia almost two hundred

Serious golfers can choose among twenty-four major golf courses, including Pipestem (left), and hikers can find trails in the state parks, in the national forests, or along the state and national scenic trails.

years ago. Charleston hosts the Vandalia Gathering, a festival of traditional West Virginia music, crafts, and culture.

Country music is the state's favorite. One of the nation's top country music radio stations is WWVA-AM, which broadcasts from Wheeling. Although Wheeling is famed as a country music center, it also is the smallest city in the nation to maintain a metropolitan-class orchestra—the highly acclaimed Wheeling Symphony.

SPORTS

The Mountain State delights active sports participants as well as fans. Outdoor sports enthusiasts can find challenges ranging from white-water rafting in the summer to cross-country skiing during the winter. A state pamphlet lists twenty-four major golf courses operating in West Virginia. Backpacking, hiking, horseback riding, and caving are among the many activities sponsored by the state

Boat racing on Bluestone Lake, in Summers County

park system. There are no major-league professional teams in West Virginia, but college and high-school teams enjoy an avid following.

The fans' devotion to the West Virginia University football team is the source of legends. The state seems to grind to a halt when the West Virginia University Mountaineers' football games are shown on television. In 1989, quarterback Major Harris became a state hero when he led the Mountaineers to the Fiesta Bowl.

West Virginia has produced many great athletes who starred in professional sports. Jack Dempsey, a heavyweight champion boxer of the 1920s, developed his muscles as a young man by working in the coalfields of Logan County. Sam Huff, an all-American linebacker for West Virginia University, became a feared defensive player for the New York Giants of the National Football League. The state's most famous athlete is Jerry West, a native of Cabin Creek. West was a sharpshooting guard for the West Virginia University basketball team and later helped the Los Angeles Lakers become a powerhouse.

Buckhannon's Strawberry Festival is an annual event.

FAIRS AND FESTIVALS

Every weekend of the year, a fun-filled festival is being held in at least one West Virginia town. Farming communities celebrate the harvest of special crops, with the Strawberry Festival at Buckhannon and the Apple Butter Festival at Berkeley Springs. Many fairs honor the state's past, such as Marlinton's Pioneer Days, which features square dancing and old-time music. Ethnic pride and an assortment of delicious food are offered at Clarksburg's Italian Heritage Festival.

The granddaddy of the state's special events is the West Virginia State Fair, held near Lewisburg every August. The State Fair draws many thousands of visitors. The state's most popular one-day event is the New River Gorge Day Festival, held in October when the fall colors are especially magical. On this special day, the bridge over the New River Gorge near Fayetteville is closed to traffic, and crowds of people are allowed to walk over it and behold the spectacular canyon carved out by the New River. The New River Gorge is just one of many natural wonders to be seen in the Mountain State.

Chapter 9.
A TOUR OF
WEST VIRGINIA

A TOUR OF WEST VIRGINIA

West Virginia offers visitors thirty-four state parks, dozens of museums and historical sites, and mile after mile of gorgeous mountain scenery. A tour of the Mountain State might begin in one of the two panhandles and continue to the southern tip.

THE EASTERN PANHANDLE

The Eastern Panhandle contains the state's best farmland. It is also the cradle of West Virginia's history, as many of the state's earliest settlements developed there.

History comes to life at Charles Town near the Virginia border. Founded in 1786, the city was named after Charles Washington, the youngest brother of George Washington. Over the generations, many members of the Washington family lived there. Charles Town's most prized structure is Harewood House, which to this day is owned by a descendant of the Washington family. In 1794, Harewood House hosted the wedding ceremony that united Dolley Payne Todd and James Madison, who became the fourth president of the United States. A historic building in the center of town is the red brick Jefferson County Courthouse, built in 1836. In this courthouse, John Brown was brought to trial. Nearby is a pyramid composed of three stones that marks the spot where John Brown was hanged.

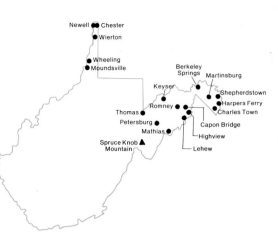

Inventor James Rumsey launched a successful steam-powered boat at Shepherdstown (left) in 1787, twenty years before Robert Fulton launched his famous *Clermont*.

Visitors to Harpers Ferry are greeted with both a sense of history and spectacular views of forestland and rushing rivers. In the town, John Brown and his abolitionist followers seized a federal arsenal, thereby pushing the nation ever closer to civil war. Harpers Ferry commemorates the famous raid with the John Brown Monument and the John Brown Museum. Just beyond the town's limits spreads the Harpers Ferry National Historical Park. Situated at the junction of the Shenandoah and Potomac rivers, the park delights hikers and picnickers.

The past is also present in Shepherdstown. At one time, George Washington proposed that Shepherdstown, then called Mecklenburg, become the nation's capital city. At Shepherdstown, in 1787, inventor James Rumsey launched a successful steam-powered boat twenty years before Robert Fulton sailed his famous *Clermont*.

Martinsburg is the Eastern Panhandle's largest city. It is a trading center for the many apple and peach growers who own nearby orchards. Martinsburg is also a shoppers' delight, famed for its many factory-outlet stores.

Smoke Hole Caverns (left) is a cave northwest of Petersburg that once was used by Indians to smoke and store meat. The historic town of Harpers Ferry (right) is an Eastern Panhandle town near the Virginia border.

The city of Berkeley Springs contains the nation's oldest health spa. Due to heat and pressure deep below the surface, the waters of the springs gush out of the ground at a soothing 74 degrees Fahrenheit (23 degrees Celsius). Thousands of visitors come each year to bathe in what they call the life-giving spring waters.

The Eastern Panhandle city of Romney, which dates to the 1760s, is one of the oldest communities in the state. Near Romney is Ice Mountain, a natural refrigerator. Crevices in the mountain are caked with ice even in the hottest summer months. Northwest of Romney is Keyser, the home of Potomac State College. To the southeast, visitors may take a lovely drive through the villages of Capon Bridge, High View, and Lehew before entering George Washington National Forest.

Farther south rise the Allegheny foothills and a wonderful world of nature. Lost River State Park, near Mathias, offers 3,712 acres (1,502 hectares) of marvelous woodlands. Visitors to the park are invited to take an invigorating hike to Cranny Crow, a high point that presents scenic vistas. Northwest of the park, near the town of Petersburg, are many fascinating caverns. The most famous of these mountain caves is Smoke Hole, which was used by Indians to smoke and store meat.

Mighty Allegheny peaks dominate eastern West Virginia. Near Riverton is Spruce Knob, the highest point in West Virginia. In the northwestern corner of the Eastern Panhandle, the town of Thomas is the gateway to Blackwater Falls State Park. There, water from the surging Blackwater Falls tumbles from an embankment as high as a five-story building.

THE NORTHERN PANHANDLE

In contrast to the Eastern Panhandle, which displays the wonders of nature, the Northern Panhandle celebrates the works of men and women. It is the state's leading industrial region.

At the top of the Northern Panhandle are the towns of Chester and Newell, both of which contain dinnerware factories. The Homer Laughlin China Company of Chester is the largest maker of plates and saucers in the world. Every weekend, shoppers searching for bargains flood the dinnerware outlet stores in the two towns.

Weirton, to the south, was founded in 1910 by Ernest T. Weir, owner of the Weirton Steel Company. In 1983, Weirton Steel was bought by its employees, and it is now the nation's largest employee-owned steel company. Many of Weirton Steel's employee-owners have European ethnic backgrounds. Once a year, the city's ethnic groups set up outdoor stands and celebrate the International Food and Arts Festival. During the festival, the scents of Greek, Polish, Italian, and German dishes fill the air, and everyone is invited to forget their diets and enjoy the feast.

Wheeling is a steel-producing city with deep roots in the state's history. On Main Street near Eleventh, a bronze plaque marks the site of Fort Henry, whose log walls once protected settlers from Indian attacks. Wheeling was also the state's first capital after West Virginia broke from Virginia. The town boasts a marvelous architectural tradition in its rows of Victorian houses, many of which have been carefully restored. Neighborhood groups sponsor walking tours through the choicest blocks of elegant old houses. A highlight of Wheeling is Oglebay Park, one of the most splendid municipal parks in the nation. In the park are golf courses, a children's zoo, a miniature train, and indoor and outdoor swimming pools.

Overlooking the Ohio River at Moundsville is the world-famous Grave Creek Mound. Built as a religious shrine some twenty-five hundred years ago, the mound greets visitors who range from curious onlookers to serious students of ancient American culture. Also at Moundsville is a modern shrine called the Palace of Gold, which was built by devotees of the Hare Krishna religion. Daily tours of the Palace of Gold allow people to view the intricate carvings in this highly unusual building.

NORTHERN WEST VIRGINIA

New Martinsville, in the northern Ohio River Valley, is an industrial center that specializes in glassworks. Shoppers come to the town's outlet stores, which sell decorative glass pieces and Tiffany-type lampshades. To the east is a town with the curious name of Hundred. Actually, the name makes sense, considering that it is derived from the longevity of two of its early settlers, Mr. and Mrs. Church. Mr. Church lived to be 109; Mrs. Church lived to be 106.

Oglebay Mansion Museum is the centerpiece of Wheeling's Oglebay Park.

Sistersville is a town with an up-and-down history. It was named for two sisters, Sarah and Delilah, who were daughters of Charles Wells, the town's founder. Until the 1890s, it was a quiet river village. Then, oil was discovered under its main street. Frantically, engineers moved houses, churches, and schools to build oil wells. The town's population zoomed from three hundred to fifteen hundred people almost overnight. When the oil wells ran dry, Sistersville returned to being a quiet village near the Ohio River. Today, its antique stores sell relics from the boom period. A little south of Sistersville is Williamstown, where master glassmakers craft decorative glass objects.

The Ohio River city of Parkersburg is known as an industrial center, but it is also a leader in culture and the arts. Lovers of fine art visit the Parkersburg Art Center to view the latest exhibits. Theatergoers pack the city's Actors Guild Playhouse, which puts on topflight dramatic and comic performances.

Tour boats out of Parkersburg stop at Blennerhassett Island, now a state park. In the late 1700s, the island was purchased by

The mansion on Blennerhassett Island has been completely reconstructed.

Harmon Blennerhassett, a wealthy Irish immigrant. He and his young wife built a handsome mansion there. The Blennerhassetts entertained many famous Americans, including Henry Clay and Johnny Appleseed. Another guest was Aaron Burr. Just after Burr shot and killed Alexander Hamilton in a pistol duel, he came to the island to meet with Blennerhassett. The two hatched a plan to build a private empire in Mexico. Many Americans regarded this empire-building scheme as an act of treason. Because of their plot, Burr lost his political future and Blennerhassett his fortune. The mansion burned down in 1811, but it has been faithfully rebuilt. Today, visitors tour the mansion while guides tell the story of its one-time owners.

Far to the east of the Ohio River is Morgantown, home of West Virginia University. The university's sprawling campus embraces 142 buildings. Its library contains the nation's largest collection of books on Appalachia. Mass transportation experts from around the country come to study Morgantown's unique Personal Rapid Transit System. In Morgantown, people are whisked around on an

Morgantown (left) boasts a unique Personal Rapid Transit System (right).

elevated, light-rail network that runs through the city. Passengers deposit their fares into slots and punch their destinations on a computerized map. No ticket takers are needed.

South of Morgantown are the cities of Fairmont and Clarksburg. A highlight in Fairmont is the One-Room School Museum—a century-old school building preserved with its original desks, books, and writing slates. Clarksburg was the birthplace of Stonewall Jackson, one of the Confederacy's most brilliant generals. A statue of Jackson stands at Courthouse Plaza in the heart of the city.

Pride in the Stonewall Jackson heritage is also displayed in the city of Weston. As a boy, Jackson worked in a Weston sawmill. Today, the Jackson's Mill Museum exhibits memorabilia of the famous general and of the Civil War era.

To the southeast lies the town of Buckhannon. Visitors there can tour the West Virginia State Wildlife Center, where more than fifty birds and animals native to the Mountain State are displayed.

The capital city of Charleston is located at the confluence of the Elk and Kanawha rivers.

CENTRAL WEST VIRGINIA

Central West Virginia is the state's heartland. It embraces large cities such as Huntington and Charleston, as well as remote river and mountain country.

Along the Ohio River is Point Pleasant, a heartland town steeped in history. Some historians argue that the first battle of the Revolutionary War took place here. They believe that the British governor of Virginia, Lord Dunmore, urged Chief Cornstalk to assail frontier settlements, thus leading to the Battle of Point Pleasant. Today, the Point Pleasant Battle Monument rises over the city's Tu-Endie-Wei Park. In the park are the graves of Chief Cornstalk and the famous Indian fighter "Mad Ann" Bailey.

The sound of cows mooing and horses neighing signals the approach to Point Pleasant's West Virginia State Farm Museum. The museum grounds have a collection of thirty farm buildings plus a one-room schoolhouse and a country store. Visitors leave with a greater understanding of the trials endured and the triumphs achieved by West Virginia farmers more than one hundred years ago.

Farther along on the southern Ohio River is Huntington, the state's second-largest city. The Huntington Museum of Art displays paintings, sculptures, and objects as diverse as Turkish prayer rugs and ancient American Indian relics. Railroad buffs come to Huntington's Heritage Village, a restored train depot. Camden Park is one of the state's most popular amusement parks. The riverboat *Camden Queen*, which is docked at Huntington, offers regular tours of the Ohio.

Charleston is the heart of the heartland. Towering above its surrounding structures is West Virginia's state capitol, one of the finest capitol buildings in the nation. Completed in 1932, the building is topped by a magnificent dome. The state capitol was designed by Cass Gilbert, a famous architect who also created the Supreme Court Building in Washington, D.C. Other architectural gems can be found in Old Charleston Village along Capitol, Summers, and Quarrier streets. The Governor's Mansion, built in the style of an old plantation house, is one of the most treasured buildings in the state. Among Charleston's attractions are the Sunrise Mansion Art Museum, the Children's Museum, and the always-popular Cultural Center, which stands next to the state capitol. In the Cultural Center is the State Museum, with displays illustrating life in the Mountain State from its Indian past to the present; the West Virginia State Theatre; and a craft shop.

Two of West Virginia's largest lakes are located in the heartland. Sutton Lake, northeast of Charleston, lures more than half a million people each year. Boat owners on Sutton Lake show off their crafts during the Regatta Festival held each year. East of Charleston, the diamond-blue waters of Summersville Lake are a favorite of scuba divers.

Almost between the two lakes, near Webster Springs, is beautiful Holly River State Park, one of West Virginia's largest.

The National Radio Astronomy Observatory in Green Bank (left) has some of the world's largest operating radio telescopes. The train at Cass Scenic Railroad State Park (right) takes visitors up Bald Knob Mountain, the second-highest peak in the state.

Experienced hikers in the park carry apples to lure the deer that sometimes lurk on the hiking trails hoping for handouts.

Near Hillsboro is Droop Mountain Battlefield State Park. On these grounds was fought the largest Civil War battle that took place in West Virginia. Events of the battle are marked so that visitors can follow the movements of the opposing armies. The great novelist Pearl S. Buck was born in the town of Hillsboro. The Nobel Award-winning author's family home has been carefully restored and is now the Pearl S. Buck Museum.

Also near Hillsboro is Watoga, West Virginia's largest state park. Cutting through the heart of the park is the lovely Greenbrier River. Hiking, swimming, and fishing make Watoga a popular wilderness playground.

Northeast of Hillsboro, in Green Bank, is the National Radio Astronomy Observatory. Radio telescopes at the observatory scan the skies seeking an answer to the age-old question: Is anyone out there? Chances are, if some civilization in deep space tries to contact earth, scientists at this mountaintop observatory will be the first to receive the message. Guided tours of the observatory are given on a regular basis.

An exciting way to see wilderness marvels is from the window of a classic steam-driven train at Cass Scenic Railroad State Park. A vacation adventure there begins at the town of Cass, which is relatively unchanged since it was created as a logging center more than a century ago. Visitors then board a train that is almost as old as the town itself. The train climbs up Bald Knob Mountain, the second-highest peak in the state. The scenery viewed from atop this lofty mountain has been described as "a bit of Canada gone astray."

THE SOUTH

More so than any other region, southern West Virginia is associated with coal. But aside from coal towns, this region has awesome wilderness attractions and ever-present reminders of the state's exciting past.

Williamson, on the Fork River, is one of the region's many coal towns. Even the walls of Williamson's Chamber of Commerce building are made of coal. In this region along the Tug Fork River, the bloody Hatfield and McCoy feud took place. To the north is the town of Logan and Chief Logan State Park, where acting companies put on an exciting summer theater program.

In Beckley, east of Logan, two interesting museums stand side by side. Visitors at the Beckley Exhibition Coal Mine board tiny railroad cars and are carried into the depths of a coal mine that was active just a few years ago. The train stops at sections where miners once blasted the coal out of the walls and shoveled it into hopper cars. Former miners act as tour guides and detail the backbreaking and dangerous chores that had to be performed in the mine. Next door is the unusual Youth Museum of Southern West Virginia, where ever-changing exhibits are designed to excite young minds.

Bramwell, to the south, is certainly not a typical coal town. During the coal industry's boom days, coal company owners lived in the town. It is estimated that fourteen millionaire coal barons owned homes in Bramwell early in the twentieth century. In the town's historic district stand striking Victorian and Tudor mansions.

Nearby Bluefield is called the nation's "air-conditioned city." Snuggled in a mountain valley that traps cold air, Bluefield remains comfortably cool even during the most sweltering summer months.

To the northeast is the magnificent New River country. The town of Hinton lies in the heart of the New River wilderness. White-water rafters push off from Hinton to take a thrilling ride over a course that includes twenty-one surging rapids. For the less daring, the New River and its branches have many quiet stretches for canoeing.

The town of Lewisburg, named the county seat of Greenbrier County in 1782, is rich in history. Its Old Stone Church was built in 1796 and still holds services today. Lewisburg's Greenbrier Historical Society Museum displays items dating from colonial America. Short drives from Lewisburg take visitors to two fascinating underground attractions—the Organ Cave and the Lost World Caverns. The Organ Cave, near Ronceverte, is the third-largest cave in the United States.

White Sulphur Springs, close to the Virginia border, is another of West Virginia's mineral-spring health spas. Famous Americans,

The restored 1898 Indian Creek Covered Bridge, a few miles southeast of Hinton, is one of West Virginia's many historic covered bridges.

including several presidents, have vacationed at White Sulphur Springs. According to a pamphlet written in 1834, the waters at White Sulphur Springs were known to cure "yellow jaundice, white swelling, black plague, fevers of every kind and color, and bad habits except for chewing, smoking, spitting, and swearing."

The town of White Sulphur Springs ends a tour of the Mountain State. Most visitors eagerly come back to West Virginia to experience once again the breathtaking mountain scenery and the friendly people. This urge to return is felt both by visitors and natives alike. It is expressed well in the refrain of John Denver's song "Take Me Home, Country Roads":

> Country roads, take me home
> To the place I belong,
> West Virginia, mountain mama,
> Take me home, country roads.

FACTS AT A GLANCE

GENERAL INFORMATION

Statehood: June 20, 1863, thirty-fifth state

Origin of Name: West Virginia was formed from the western counties of the state of Virginia, which was named for Elizabeth, the Virgin Queen of England.

State Capital: Charleston, capital since 1885

State Nicknames: Mountain State and Panhandle State

State Flag: The flag consists of a white field bordered by blue with the design from the state seal in the center, wreathed by rhododendron leaves. A banner with the words "State of West Virginia" is found above the seal, which depicts a farmer and a miner. Between them is a large, ivy-draped rock bearing the date of West Virginia's admission to the Union. In front of the rock are two hunter's rifles upon which rests a cap of liberty.

State Motto: *Montani Semper Liberi* (Mountaineers Are Always Free)

State Bird: Cardinal

State Flower: Rhododendron

State Tree: Sugar maple

State Animal: Black bear

State Fish: Brook trout

State Colors: Blue and gold

State Song: "The West Virginia Hills," words by Ellen King and music by
H. E. Engle:

> Oh, the West Virginia hills!
> How majestic and how grand,
> With their summits bathed in glory,
> Like our Prince Immanuel's land!
> Is it any wonder then,
> That my heart with rapture thrills,
> As I stand once more with loved ones
> On those West Virginia hills?
>
> Oh the hills,
> Beautiful hills.
> How I love the West Virginia hills!
> If o'er sea or land I roam
> Still I'll think of happy home,
> And the friends among the West Virginia hills.

POPULATION

Population: 1,950,258, thirty-fourth among the states (1980 census)

Population Density: 80 persons per sq. mi. (31 persons per km²)

Population Distribution: West Virginia is a far less urban state than most. Only
36 percent of the state's people live in cities or towns. Only nine cities had more
than 20,000 persons in 1980. Charleston, the state capital, is the largest city.

Charleston	63,968
Huntington	63,684
Wheeling	43,070
Parkersburg	39,946
Morgantown	27,605
Weirton	25,371
Fairmont	23,863
Clarksburg	22,371
Beckley	20,492
Bluefield	16,060

(Population figures according to 1980 census)

Population Growth: Few states are as dependent on unstable industries as West
Virginia. The coal industry for years determined the state's prosperity or poverty.
When coal prices were high, the state saw steady population growth. But when the
industry became unsteady, people left in droves to seek work elsewhere. Thus,
West Virginia was the only state in the Union to lose population between 1950 and
1970. Although the Mountain State made some gains during the 1970s and early

Eagle Rock, at the South Branch of the Potomac River

1980s, it is again losing population and appears doomed to lose a representative in Congress after the 1990 redistricting. The list below shows population growth in West Virginia since 1870:

Year	Population
1870	442,014
1880	618,457
1900	958,800
1910	1,221,119
1920	1,463,701
1930	1,729,205
1940	1,901,974
1950	2,005,552
1960	1,860,421
1970	1,744,237
1980	1,950,258

GEOGRAPHY

Borders: States that border West Virginia are Ohio on the northwest, Pennsylvania and Maryland on the north, Virginia on the east and south, and Kentucky on the southwest.

Highest Point: Spruce Knob, in Pendleton County, 4,863 ft. (1,482 m) above sea level

111

Lowest Point: The Potomac River in Jefferson County, 240 ft. (73 m) above sea level

Greatest Distances: North to south—237 mi. (381 km)
East to west—265 mi. (426 km)

Area: 24,231 sq. mi. (62,758 km²)

Rank in Area Among the States: Forty-first

National Forests and Parklands: Monongahela National Forest covers 840,000 acres (339,940 hectares) in Randolph, Tucker, Pocahontas, and adjoining counties. It includes the spectacular 63-ft. (19-m) Blackwater Falls in Blackwater Canyon, limestone caverns, and the Cranberry Glades. Parts of George Washington and Jefferson national forests are also located in West Virginia. The Spruce Knob-Seneca Rocks National Recreation Area also lures thousands of tourists each year, as does Harpers Ferry National Historical Park.

Rivers: A number of rivers flow along West Virginia's borders, giving the state its unusual shape. Most important of these is the Ohio, which forms the western boundary for 275 mi. (442 km) and gives West Virginia access to the Mississippi River system. The Big Sandy River forms the other part of the western border. Other rivers that flow into the Ohio River include the Little Kanawha and the New and Gauley rivers, which join to form the Kanawha River. The Monongahela, which joins the Allegheny in Pittsburgh to form the Ohio, has its source in West Virginia. The Potomac, the most important of the rivers that flow into Chesapeake Bay, also has its source in West Virginia. The Potomac forms the northern border of the Eastern Panhandle. The Shenandoah, a river celebrated in story and song, flows into the Potomac.

Lakes: West Virginia has no large natural lakes. Locks and dams have created reservoirs that serve as lakes. The largest of these reservoirs is 4-sq.-mi. (10-km²) Summersville Lake, on the Gauley River. Others include Sutton Lake, on the Elk River; Bluestone Lake, on the New River; Tygart Lake, on the Tygart River; and East Lynn Lake, on Twelvepole Creek.

Topography: Some states have deceptive nicknames. The only diamonds in Delaware are in jewelry stores. Illinois is losing its once-vast prairies. Most lifelong Michigan residents have never seen a wolverine. But West Virginia continues to earn the nickname Mountain State. West Virginians like to boast that if their state were ironed out, it would cover the entire country. Mean elevation in West Virginia is 1,500 ft. (457 m), the highest of any state east of the Mississippi.
West Virginia contains three major land divisions. The Appalachian Plateau covers the western 80 percent of the state. Most of the state's natural resources can be found here, as well as most of its people. It descends southwestward from Pennsylvania in a series of ridges. Streams cut narrow valleys into these ridges, leaving flat-topped uplands and rounded hills.
The Allegheny Front, a steep wall of mountains, divides the Appalachian Plateau from the eastern part of the state. This eastern region is known as the Appalachian

Autumn in Canaan Valley Resort State Park

Ridge and Valley region (or Great Appalachian Valley). These mountains are made of folded layers of sedimentary rock. Heavily forested ridges are separated by narrow valleys that provide rich soil.

A tip of the Eastern Panhandle lies in the Blue Ridge region, mountains formed from igneous and metamorphic rocks. Apple and peach orchards grow in this region's fertile soil.

Climate: West Virginia's different altitudes cause climatic variations. Charleston, in a river valley, has average January temperatures between 27° and 46° F. (-3° and 8° C) and July average temperatures between 64° and 87° F. (18° and 31° C). Elkins, at a higher elevation, has January averages of 22° to 43° F. (-6° to 6° C) and July temperatures from 57° to 83° F. (14° to 28° C).

Rainfall is plentiful in all parts of the state, but is generally heavier in the southern mountains than the Potomac River area. Heavy winter and spring floods are not uncommon in the lower valleys. Thick fog often covers these valleys. Snowfall varies from 20 in. (51 cm) in the southwest to 100 in. (254 cm) in the mountains.

NATURE

Trees: Oaks, hemlocks, red spruces, white pines, sycamores, locusts, hickories, ashes, maples, walnuts, beeches, chestnuts, elms, birches, mulberries, yellow poplars, aspens, gums, cherry trees, tulip trees

Wild Plants: Bloodroots, hepaticas, dogwoods, azaleas, rhododendrons, asters, black-eyed Susans, goldenrod, coltsfoot, sundews, bog rosemaries, kalmias, wisterias, box huckleberries

Animals: White-tailed deer, black bears, gray and red foxes, minks, opossums, raccoons, skunks, beavers, wildcats, martens, groundhogs, frogs, toads, snakes, turtles

Hawks (above) and bald eagles (right) are among the birds that can be seen in West Virginia.

Birds: Wild turkeys, ruffed grouses, bobwhites, great horned owls, hawks, eagles, cardinals, tufted titmice, scarlet tanagers, catbirds, blackbirds, crows, wrens, sparrows

Fish: Tuna, bass, pike, bluefish, carp, catfish, sucker, walleye, trout

GOVERNMENT

West Virginia adopted its first constitution at statehood in 1863. The second, and present, constitution, adopted in 1872, has been amended more than fifty times. Amendments may be proposed in either house of the legislature, but must be approved by a two-thirds majority of both houses and then by a majority of the voters. A constitutional convention may be called to change the constitution, but it must be approved by a majority of the legislature and the voters.

The Mountain State's government, like the federal government, is composed of three branches. The legislative branch consists of a senate and a house of delegates who meet each year to pass laws. The thirty-four senators, elected from seventeen senatorial districts, serve four-year terms. The one hundred delegates serve two-year terms. West Virginia has thirty-six delegate districts, each of which elects from one to thirteen delegates.

West Virginia's governor, elected to a four-year term, heads the executive branch. The governor may not serve more than two consecutive terms. Voters also elect the secretary of state, auditor, treasurer, attorney general, and commissioner of agriculture to four-year terms. Directors of other state departments are appointed by the governor.

The supreme court of appeals is the highest court in the state's judicial system. Its five judges are elected to twelve-year terms, and they choose a chief justice from among their members. West Virginia is divided into thirty-one judicial districts. Each has a circuit court with one or more judges elected to eight-year terms. Every West Virginia county also has one or more magistrate courts. These judges are elected to four-year terms.

Number of Counties: 55

U.S. Representatives: 4

Electoral Votes: 6

Voting Qualifications: U.S. citizen, eighteen years of age, registered to vote thirty days before an election

EDUCATION

Public education did not begin immediately in the areas now part of West Virginia, because parents felt they were responsible only for their own children's education. Early schools were private, supported by parent subscription. Parents paid the teachers in cash, produce, or bed and board. In 1796, Virginia passed a law providing for free district schools in counties that wished to establish them. An 1810 Virginia law created a literary fund for the education of poor children.

West Virginia, upon joining the Union, established a system of free schools. Nine years later, a new constitution provided the funds to support those schools. In 1890, the Wade Plan, named after educator Alexander L. Wade, developed a method for teaching subjects at different grade levels to different children.

A nine-member board of education, appointed by the governor to nine-year terms, now determines educational policies. The board appoints a superintendent of schools, who supervises public education. Children from ages seven through fifteen must attend school.

The state has about 358,000 students in public elementary schools, with another 12,000 or so in private schools. Expenditure per pupil in the public schools is about $3,000 per year.

West Virginia did not have public high schools until 1908. Before that time, only private schools provided secondary education. Now the state has about 112,000 students in public secondary schools.

State-supported colleges and universities include West Virginia University, at Morgantown; Marshall University, at Huntington; Bluefield State College, at Bluefield; Concord College, at Athens; Fairmont State College, at Fairmont; Glenville State College, at Glenville; Shepherd College, at Shepherdstown; West Liberty State College, at West Liberty; West Virginia Institute of Technology, at Montgomery; and West Virginia State College, at Institute. Private colleges include Alderson-Broaddus College, at Philippi; Bethany College, at Bethany; Davis and Elkins College, at Elkins; the University of Charleston, at Charleston; Salem

Livestock, including Yorkshire pigs (above), provides much of the state's farm income.

College, at Salem; Ohio Valley College, at Parkersburg; West Virginia Wesleyan College, at Buckhannon; and Wheeling Jesuit College, at Wheeling.

ECONOMY AND INDUSTRY

Principal Products:
Agriculture: Dairy products, livestock, hay, corn, vegetables, tobacco, poultry, sheep, potatoes, grapes, apples, peaches, strawberries, oats, buckwheat, hogs, barley, wheat

Manufacturing: Dyes, detergents, paints, plastics, synthetic rubber, steel, tin, glassware, bottles, pottery, chinaware, tile, mining machinery, railroad cars

Natural Resources: Coal, salt, clay, oil, natural gas, forest products, stone, sand, gravel

Business and Trade: For years, the often dangerous but highly profitable coal industry was the lifeblood of West Virginia's economy. Coal still reigns as an important West Virginia product. On average, the state produces about 130 million tons (118 million metric tons) a year. Cities such as Beckley, Bluefield, Fairmont, Welch, and Williamson owe their development to the coal industry. The Mountain State led the nation in coal production from 1936 to 1974, when it was surpassed by Kentucky. Now that economy is diversifying.

Manufacturing provides another important source of income. Chemicals and related products, including dyes, detergents, paints, plastics, and rubber, are the most important industries. Blast furnaces at Wheeling and Weirton produce many iron and steel products. West Virginia also enjoys a reputation for its high-quality pottery and glassware.

Even though most of the original West Virginia settlers were farmers and herders, agriculture is no longer one of the state's major sources of income. In recent years, agriculture has provided less than 0.5 percent of the gross state product. Livestock and dairy goods are the most important agricultural commodities. Orchards produce large amounts of apples and peaches.

116

Wheeling, located on the Ohio River, is a commercial center that once rivaled Pittsburgh. It still serves as a major river port. Charleston, on the Kanawha River, is the state's leading center for wholesale and retail trade. Huntington is also a major trade center because of its river and railroad traffic.

Communication: In 1790, the *Potomak Guardian and Berkeley Advertiser* in Shepherdstown started as the first newspaper in what is now West Virginia. Ten years later, another Shepherdstown paper, the *Roane County Reporter*, the state's oldest continuous newspaper, began. Now West Virginia has about 75 newspapers, including about 25 dailies. Leading newspapers include the *Charleston Gazette*, the *Charleston Daily Mail*, the *Huntington Herald-Dispatch*, and the *Wheeling News-Register*. WSAZ in Huntington began operations in 1923 as the state's first radio station. Today, about 100 radio stations cover the state. WSAZ-TV began broadcasting in 1949. West Virginia has 12 television stations.

Transportation: Rivers were the first highways in what is now West Virginia, and even today they serve as major freight routes. The Ohio, Monongahela, Kanawha, and Big Sandy rivers serve as major providers of transportation.

The first railroad, the Baltimore & Ohio, reached Wheeling in 1853. By 1920, almost every county had rail service. Now fifteen railroads operate on about 4,000 mi. (6,437 km) of track. Ten cities receive passenger service.

West Virginia has about 35,000 mi. (56,326 km) of roads and highways. Interstate 77 crosses the western part of the state, from Williamstown to Bluefield. Its route from Charleston to Princeton forms the West Virginia Turnpike, the state's only important toll road. Interstate 64 passes from Charleston to Huntington and west to Kentucky. Interstate 70 cuts through the Northern Panhandle at Wheeling. Interstate 79 connects Charleston with Morgantown.

Charleston, with four domestic airlines, is the state's aviation hub. West Virginia has about forty-five airports, most of them private facilities.

SOCIAL AND CULTURAL LIFE

Museums: West Virginians have the opportunity to enjoy a number of varied museums. Local art lovers boast of the Huntington Museum of Art, in Huntington, with collections of American, British, and French paintings, Turkish rugs, and pre-Columbian artifacts. West Virginia State College holds an Asian art collection in its library. Other art museums include the Parkersburg Art Center, in Parkersburg, and the Oglebay Institute-Mansion Museum, in Wheeling. The Sunrise Foundation, at Charleston, has an art gallery, a children's museum, and a planetarium. The Cultural Center in Charleston's Capitol Complex houses a library, archives, and exhibits that include a settler's cabin, a country store, and a Civil War display. Exhibits at the Master Armorer's House in Harpers Ferry describe the history of gun making. The Pocahontas County Historical Museum, in Marlinton, contains documents, implements, clothes, and toys. Marshall University, in Huntington, has a geology museum. Alexander Fine Arts Center, at Concord College in Princeton, has a notable pipe organ, a theater, and an art gallery.

The Sunrise Museum complex, at Charleston, includes an art gallery, a children's museum, and a planetarium.

Libraries: The counties in present-day West Virginia had subscription libraries as early as 1808. The first public library opened about 1900, and a state library began operation in 1929. Today, about 170 public library systems operate in most of the state's fifty-five counties. Bookmobiles serve the rural areas. The state's largest library, located at West Virginia University, contains the West Virginia Regional History Collection of manuscripts and books. The Division of Culture and History, at Charleston, contains an archives section with an extensive collection of public records, official reports, and other historical materials.

Performing Arts: Music and theater have been a staple of West Virginia ever since the earliest settlements. Bluegrass banjo players and fiddlers stir hearts from Wheeling to Bluefield to Harpers Ferry. West Virginia enjoys many folk-music festivals throughout the state and throughout the year. West Virginia also has larger events. Charleston and Wheeling boast symphony orchestras. Charleston has a Children's Theater. Wheeling's Little Theater Group gives open-air performances. Grandview State Park presents two regular outdoor performances: *Honey in the Rock*, a play dealing with West Virginia statehood, and *The Hatfields and the McCoys*, based on the famous feud between the two families.

Sports and Recreation: One Saturday every autumn, the state of West Virginia virtually comes to a standstill. That is the day when the West Virginia University (WVU) Mountaineers play their archrival, the University of Pittsburgh Panthers. The Mountaineers have fared well in the series recently, and against most other teams as well. West Virginia, led by quarterback Major Harris, finished the 1988 regular season undefeated, losing the unofficial national championship to Notre Dame in the 1989 Fiesta Bowl. Over the years, WVU has produced many stars for professional teams. Sam Huff crushed opposing runners as a linebacker for the New York Giants. Basketball's Jerry West sank outside shots for more than a decade with the Los Angeles Lakers.

West Virginians also enjoy the active, outdoor life. They hike, camp, fish, and swim in the state's thirty-four state parks and nine state forests. Hunting, golf, and tennis are other popular activities. The more adventurous enjoy white-water rafting on fast, rushing streams such as the New River.

Historic Sites and Landmarks:

Andrews Methodist Church, in Grafton, is known as the International Mother's Day Shrine. Anna Jarvis, who taught Sunday school there, developed the idea of Mother's Day. Her work led to Congress declaring the second Sunday in May as Mother's Day.

Blennerhassett Island State Park, on the Ohio River near Parkersburg, was the site of a large mansion built by Harmon Blennerhassett, who was accused with Aaron Burr of plotting an independent government in the Southwest. The house was destroyed by fire in 1811 but has been completely rebuilt.

Campbell Mansion, in Bethany, is the twenty-seven-room restored home of Alexander Campbell, the founder of the Disciples of Christ church and of Bethany College.

Charles Town, founded by George Washington's youngest brother, Charles, was the site of John Brown's trial.

Covered Bridge, near Philippi, was the site of the first Civil War battle in West Virginia. It is one of six two-lane covered bridges still standing in the United States.

Droop Mountain Battlefield State Park, near Hillsboro, preserves the land where Union troops destroyed the last major rebel resistance in the state.

Grave Creek Mound, in Moundsville, is the tallest prehistoric burial mound in the United States.

Harewood House, near Charles Town, was built in 1770 as the home of George Washington's brother Samuel.

Harper House, in Harpers Ferry, is the town's oldest surviving structure, dating from 1775.

Harpers Ferry National Historical Park, south of Harpers Ferry, preserves most of the original town of Harpers Ferry, which was taken over by abolitionist John Brown in an antislavery raid in 1859. Included in the park are the *Master Armorer's House*, *John Brown's Fort*, *Harper House*, and *Lockwood House*.

Jackson's Mill, near Weston, was the family farm where Confederate general Thomas "Stonewall" Jackson spent many summers as a boy.

Morgan Monument, in Bunker Hill, honors the state's first white settler, Morgan ap Morgan.

The Old Stone Church, in Lewisburg, was built in 1796.

Old Stone Presbyterian Church, in Lewisburg, was built of native limestone in 1796 by Scotch-Irish settlers.

Rumsey Memorial Monument, in Shepherdstown, commemorates a steam-propelled boat piloted by James Rumsey in 1787.

West Virginia Independence Hall-Customs House, in Wheeling, marks the site where West Virginia declared its independence from Virginia during the Civil War.

Other Interesting Places to Visit:

Americana Museum, in Aurora, includes an old-time doctor's office, a country store, a kitchen, a blacksmith shop, a parlor, and a bedroom.

Beckley Exhibition Coal Mine, in Beckley, shows the operations of a real coal mine.

Berkeley Springs State Park, in Berkeley Springs, is the oldest health spa in the nation, with waters that were praised by George Washington.

Pearl S. Buck Museum, in Hillsboro, marks the birthplace of the renowned writer.

Cass Scenic Railroad, in Cass, is a steam-driven locomotive that takes visitors up Bald Knob Mountain for an extraordinary view of the surrounding mountains.

Governor's Mansion, in Charleston, is an elegant Georgian-revival structure of red Harvard brick and white Corinthian columns.

Jamboree USA, at Capitol Music Hall in Wheeling, is a presentation of live country-music shows by WWVA radio.

The Governor's Mansion

National Radio Astronomy Observatory, in Green Bank, is a national center for the study of radio waves from space.

Old Green Hill Cemetery, in Martinsburg, is patterned after a Parisian cemetery. Confederate and Union soldiers, Belle Boyd's parents, and David Hunter Strother are buried there.

Oldest Living Things, an area near White Sulphur Springs, includes plants that some biologists believe are six thousand years old.

Organ Cave, near Lewisburg, was once used by Robert E. Lee as an ammunition depot. One of the stalactite formations, which looks like organ pipes, makes musical notes when struck.

The Point, near Harpers Ferry, marks the intersection of three states—West Virginia, Virginia, and Maryland—and the confluence of the Shenandoah and Potomac rivers.

Seneca Rocks National Recreation Area, in Pendleton County, contains many colorful layers of rock and stands 1,000 ft. (305 m) above the surrounding valley.

Smoke Hole Caverns, near Petersburg, is a cave that was used by Seneca Indians to smoke and store meat. During the Civil War, ammunition was stored there.

State Capitol, in Charleston, built in the Italian Renaissance style, has a dome that rises 300 ft. (91 m) above the street and a chandelier weighing more than 2 tons (1.8 metric tons).

West Virginia Wesleyan College, in Buckhannon, has a chapel that houses an organ with 1,474 pipes.

IMPORTANT DATES

15,000 B.C.—First Indians arrive in what is now West Virginia

1000 B.C.-A.D. 1000—Hopewell and Adena Indians develop a mound-building culture

1606—King James grants a charter to the London Company for land that includes what is now the state of West Virginia

1669-70—John Lederer and companions become the first Virginians to see West Virginia

1671—Thomas Batts and Robert Fallam lead an expedition across the Blue Ridge and Allegheny mountains to the New River

1712—Baron Christopher de Graffenreid visits what is now the Eastern Panhandle seeking land for Swiss families

1727—Germans from Pennsylvania establish a settlement at Mecklenburg, now Shepherdstown

1731?—Morgan ap Morgan, the area's first white settler, builds a log cabin at Bunker Hill

1742—John Peter Salley discovers coal on the Coal River

1747—George Washington surveys western Virginia lands for Lord Fairfax and discovers the warm springs at Bath, now Berkeley Springs

1755—Troops led by General Edward Braddock and George Washington march through western Virginia on their way to Pittsburgh, where they are defeated by the French and the Indians

1757—Hampshire County, the first county in present-day West Virginia, is formed

1768—The Cherokee and Iroquois give up all claim to lands between the Allegheny Mountains and the Ohio River

1773—The first permanent settlement is made in the Kanawha Valley

1774—Settlers fight the Shawnees at the Battle of Point Pleasant in Lord Dunmore's War

1776—Settlers in western Virginia first petition Virginia for their own government

1789—Daniel Boone is commissioned a lieutenant of the Kanawha (western Virginia) militia

1794—Peter Tarr builds the first iron furnace west of the Allegheny Mountains at King's Creek in the Northern Panhandle; Indians retreat across the Ohio River

1815—Natural gas is discovered near Charleston

1830—A new Virginia constitution gives few concessions to the western counties

1841—William Tompkins first uses natural gas as a fuel in the manufacture of salt

1851—Joseph Johnson of Bridgeport, the only Virginia governor to come from the western counties, takes office

1859—John Brown and his followers raid the federal arsenal at Harpers Ferry; Brown is convicted of treason and is hanged at Charles Town

1860—The first oil well begins operation at Burning Springs

1861—The counties of western Virginia refuse to secede from the Union with Virginia and propose the separate state of West Virginia; Confederates retreat from Rich Mountain

1863—West Virginia enters the Union as the thirty-fifth state, with Wheeling as its capital

1866—West Virginia refuses to reunite with Virginia after the close of the Civil War

1870—Charleston becomes the capital of West Virginia

1871—The legislature repeals a law denying voting rights to former Confederate soldiers; a lawsuit by Virginia to recover Berkeley and Jefferson counties is unsuccessful

1872—West Virginia ratifies the present state constitution

1875—West Virginia's capital shifts back to Wheeling

1877—A railroad strike at Martinsburg ignites workers throughout the nation to action

1881—Nathan Goff, of Clarksburg, becomes secretary of the navy

1885—The capital is moved back to Charleston, where it remains

1889—Oil strikes lead to a boom in the Mannington area

1890—The United Mine Workers of America union begins organizing West Virginia's workers

1891—The Hatfield and McCoy feud ends after several generations and dozens of killings; West Virginia's Stephen B. Elkins, one of the nation's most powerful Republicans, is appointed secretary of war under President Benjamin Harrison

1904—West Virginia industrialist Henry G. Davis seeks the vice-presidency as the running mate of Alton B. Parker, but the Democratic ticket loses the election to Theodore Roosevelt

1915—The United States Supreme Court rules that West Virginia owes Virginia $12,393,929.50 as part of the state debt at the time of its separation from Virginia

1920—Margaret Prescott Montague wins the O. Henry Memorial Prize for her short story "England to America"

1921—Striking miners fight federal troops for four days at the Battle of Blair Mountain; West Virginia becomes the first state to levy a sales tax; the state capitol is destroyed by fire

1924—West Virginia native John W. Davis wins the Democratic nomination for the presidency after a record 102 ballots, but loses a landslide election to Republican Calvin Coolidge; Howard Gore becomes U.S. secretary of agriculture

1932—Pearl S. Buck wins the Pulitzer Prize in fiction for *The Good Earth*

1938—Pearl S. Buck wins the Nobel Prize in literature

1939—West Virginia completes payment of its debt to Virginia

1943—Vast salt deposits are discovered in the northwestern part of the state

1946—Major chemical facilities begin operating on the Ohio River

1947—Chuck Yeager, of Myra, becomes the first pilot to fly faster than the speed of sound

1959—The National Radio Astronomy Observatory begins operations at Green Bank

1960—John F. Kennedy wins an important Democratic primary election in West Virginia, thus proving that a Roman Catholic candidate can win in a state with a Protestant majority

1965—The West Virginia legislature abolishes capital punishment and passes laws to control strip mining and water and air pollution

1968—Explosions and fires in a Farmington coal mine take seventy-eight lives, leading to new mine-safety laws; George Crumb, Jr., of Charleston, wins the Pulitzer Prize in music for *Echoes of Time in the River*

1972—A huge flood kills more than one hundred persons near Man; Arch Moore, Jr., the first West Virginia governor eligible for reelection, wins a second term

1976—Robert Byrd becomes majority leader of the United States Senate; John D. (Jay) Rockefeller IV wins the election as governor after spending $10 million on his campaign

1986—Byrd once again becomes the Senate majority leader, the first senator ever to lose, then regain, the position

1988—The West Virginia Mountaineers complete an undefeated regular football season, but lose the unofficial national championship to Notre Dame in the Fiesta Bowl

IMPORTANT PEOPLE

Newton Diehl Baker (1871-1937), born in Martinsburg; politician; contributed to the movement to get Woodrow Wilson the 1912 Democratic nomination and the presidency; secretary of war (1916-21); prepared the expedition that pursued Pancho Villa in Mexico; selected John Pershing as commander of the Allied Expeditionary Forces (AEF) in World War I

NEWTON D. BAKER

Daniel Boone (1734-1820), explorer and scout; lived at Clendenin's Settlement, forerunner of present-day Charleston; served in the county militia and in the Virginia assembly from Kanawha County; as a settler in Kentucky, he opened up the area beyond the Appalachian Mountains to settlement

Arthur Ingram Boreman (1823-1896), politician; first governor of West Virginia (1863-69); opposed Virginia's secession from the Union; presided at the second Wheeling convention, which voted for the separation of West Virginia from Virginia; U.S. senator (1869-75)

DANIEL BOONE

BELLE BOYD

PEARL BUCK

ROBERT C. BYRD

JOHNSON N. CAMDEN

Belle Boyd (1843-1900), born in Martinsburg; author, actress, Confederate spy; was captured and released three times by Union troops; described her adventures in her book *Belle Boyd in Camp and Prison*; later lectured and performed as an actress in England and the United States

George Brett (1953-   ), born in Glen Dale; professional baseball player; won two American League batting championships with the Kansas City Royals; won the 1980 Most Valuable Player Award, when he led the Royals to the American League pennant; led the Royals to their 1985 World Series victory

John Brown (1800-1859), abolitionist whose attempts to free the slaves helped hasten the Civil War; worked to keep Kansas from becoming a slave state by attacking proslavery settlers; raided the U.S. arsenal at Harpers Ferry; was tried, convicted of treason, and hanged at Charles Town for the raid on Harpers Ferry

Pearl Sydenstricker Buck (1892-1973), born in Hillsboro; author; wrote novels about her experiences in China; won the 1932 Pulitzer Prize in fiction for *The Good Earth*; won the 1938 Nobel Prize in literature; also wrote *East Wind, West Wind; Dragon Seed;* and *The Living Reed*

Selva Lewis "Lew" Burdette (1926-   ), born in Nitro; professional baseball player; pitched many years for the Milwaukee (now Atlanta) Braves; won more than 200 career games; starred in the 1957 World Series when he beat the New York Yankees three times, including two shutouts

Jesse Cail Burkett (1868-1953), born in Wheeling; professional baseball player; batted .400 or better three times in his career; won three National League batting titles for the Cleveland Spiders and the St. Louis Cardinals; entered the Baseball Hall of Fame (1946)

Robert C. Byrd (1917-   ), politician; U.S. senator from West Virginia (1959-   ); Senate majority leader (1977-81, 1987-89); became noted for his hard work, his mastery of Senate detail, and his country fiddle playing; won reelection to the Senate five times with the greatest margins of votes in West Virginia history

Johnson Newlon Camden (1828-1908), born near Braxton County; industrialist, politician; developed the state's railroad and oil industries; pioneered oil production at Burning Springs; U.S. senator from West Virginia (1881-87, 1893-95)

Alexander Campbell (1788-1866), minister; founded the Disciples of Christ church; president of Bethany College (1840-66); published the *Christian Baptist*, the first religious publication in West Virginia

Bernie Casey (1939-　　), born in Wyco; professional football player, actor; played football with the San Francisco 49ers (1961-66) and the Los Angeles Rams (1967-68); starred in "Love Is Not Enough," a television series dealing with a loving black family

Cornstalk (1720?-1777), Shawnee chief; led Shawnee forces against Virginia troops in the Battle of Point Pleasant

George Henry Crumb, Jr. (1929-　　), born in Charleston; composer; won the 1968 Pulitzer Prize in music for *Echoes of Time in the River*; used unusual musical instruments such as gongs, musical saws, and toy pianos in his pieces

Phyllis Curtin (1922-　　), born in Clarksburg; operatic soprano; interpreted the works of Mozart, Verdi, and Richard Strauss; appeared with the New England Opera Company, the New York City Opera, and the Metropolitan Opera

Dagmar (1926-　　), born Jennie Lewis in Huntington; comedienne; satirized Hollywood actresses on the early television show "Broadway Open House"; appeared as a regular contestant on the game show "Masquerade Party"

Elliot Daingerfield (1859-1932), born in Harpers Ferry; artist; drew figure studies and landscapes that became known in America and abroad; created *My Lady Rhododendron, Planting, The Lost Sheep,* and *The Tanagra*

Henry Gassaway Davis (1823-1916), industrialist, politician; built railroads connecting Charleston and Elkins to Cumberland, Maryland; ran as the unsuccessful vice-presidential candidate with Alton B. Parker against Theodore Roosevelt in 1904; U.S. senator (1871-83)

John William Davis (1873-1955), born in Clarksburg; lawyer, politician; U.S. representative (1911-13); U.S. solicitor general (1913-18); advised the American delegation at the Paris peace talks after World War I; U.S. ambassador to Great Britain (1918-21); won the 1924 Democratic nomination for president after 102 ballots, but lost in a landslide election to Calvin Coolidge; argued more cases before the Supreme Court than any other attorney in history

Joseph H. Diss Debar (1820-1905), lived in Doddridge County; artist; designed West Virginia's state seal and coat of arms; compiled the first *Handbook of West Virginia*

Martin Robinson Delany (1812-1885), born in Charleston; abolitionist, physician, soldier; with Frederick Douglass, founded *The North Star* newspaper (1847); was the first black major in the U.S. Army (1865)

Joanne Dru (1923-　　), born Joanne LaCock in Logan; actress; starred in the early television comedy "Guestward, Ho!" and in movies such as *Red River* and *She Wore a Yellow Ribbon*

BERNIE CASEY

ELLIOT DAINGERFIELD

JOHN W. DAVIS

MARTIN R. DELANY

WILLIAM H. HARVEY

SAM HUFF

STONEWALL JACKSON

JOHN KNOWLES

Thomas Ewing (1789-1871), born near West Liberty; lawyer, politician; U.S. secretary of the treasury (1841); first U.S. secretary of the interior (1849-50); U.S. senator from Ohio (1831-37, 1850-51)

John Wesley "Jack" Glasscock (1859-1947), born in Wheeling; professional baseball player; won the 1890 National League batting championship with the New York (now San Francisco) Giants; retired with 2,040 hits and a .290 batting average

William Hope "Coin" Harvey (1851-1936), born in Buffalo; economist, pamphleteer; fought for free coinage of silver; wrote *Coin's Financial School*, *A Tale of Two Nations*, and *Coin on Money, Trusts, and Imperialism*

C. E. Haworth (1860-1929), born in Huntington; composer; wrote *Te Deum* and *Jubilante*; his works are often played during Episcopal church services

Robert Lee "Sam" Huff (1934-), born in Edna Gas; professional football player; a star linebacker for the New York Giants (1956-63) and the Washington Redskins (1964-67, 1969); led the Giants to three division titles and one National Football League championship; entered the Professional Football Hall of Fame (1982)

Thomas "Stonewall" Jackson (1824-1863), born in Clarksburg; Confederate general; won against overwhelming odds at the First Battle of Bull Run; defeated Union troops in a series of lightning marches; was accidentally killed by one of his own men at Chancellorsville

Anna Jarvis (1864-1948), born in Grafton; promoter; successfully worked to establish Mother's Day as a national holiday

Louis A. Johnson (1891-1966), lawyer, government official; practiced law in Clarksburg; National Commander of the American Legion (1932-33); secretary of defense (1949-50)

John Edward Kenna (1848-1893), born in St. Albans; politician; led the campaign to make Charleston the permanent state capital; helped improve navigation on the Kanawha River; U.S. representative (1876-83); U.S. senator (1883-93); represents West Virginia in the U.S. Capitol's Statuary Hall

Don Knotts (1924-), born in Morgantown; actor; starred for years as the nervous deputy Barney Fife in "The Andy Griffith Show," for which he won an Emmy (1961); also starred in "The Don Knotts Show," "The Steve Allen Show," and "Three's Company"

John Knowles (1926-), born in Fairmont; novelist; wrote *A Separate Peace* (1960), now a favorite novel of many college students; demonstrated complex, thoughtful plots in books such as *Spreading Fires*, *Phineas*, and *The Paragon*

Karl Spencer Lashley (1890-1958), born in Davis; psychologist; studied the functions of the brain in relation to human behavior; director of the Yerkes Primate Research Center (1942-55)

Gino Marchetti (1927-   ), born in Smithers; professional football player; appeared in eleven straight Pro Bowl games as a defensive end with the Baltimore Colts; led the Colts to NFL titles in 1958 and 1959; was selected one of the greatest NFL defensive ends in the league's first fifty years; entered the Professional Football Hall of Fame (1982)

George Preston Marshall (1896-1969), born in Charleston; football owner; shifted the Boston Redskins to Washington and helped make it one of professional football's most successful franchises; promoted rule changes to help passing and field goals; a charter member of the Professional Football Hall of Fame (1963)

GEORGE P. MARSHALL

Peter Marshall (1927-   ), born Pierre LaCock in Huntington; television personality; hosted the television quiz show "Hollywood Squares"

William Stanley "Bill" Mazeroski (1936-   ), born in Wheeling; professional baseball player; starred for seventeen years as a second baseman for the Pittsburgh Pirates; played in seven All-Star games; hit the home run that won the 1960 World Series for Pittsburgh

PETER MARSHALL

Charles McCoy (1941-   ), born in Oak Hill; musician; played harmonica and directed music for the popular television show "Hee Haw"

John McKay (1923-   ), born in Everettsville; football coach; directed the University of Southern California Trojans to 127 victories in sixteen years, winning nine conference titles and four national championships; first coach of the Tampa Bay Buccaneers (1976)

Eleazer Hutchinson Miller (1831-1921), born in Shepherdstown; artist; won fame as an etcher and illustrator of such books as *Tam O'Shanter* and *Song of the Sea*

JOHN McKAY

Margaret Prescott Montague (1878-1955), born in White Sulphur Springs; author; wrote short stories depicting mountain life; received the 1920 O. Henry Memorial Prize for "England to America"; wrote "In Calvert's Valley," "Linda," "Up Eel River," and "The Lucky Lady"

Arch A. Moore, Jr. (1923-   ), born in Moundsville; politician; governor (1969-77, 1985-89); claimed credit for many new jobs and lower taxes; called for increased spending for higher education

Morgan ap Morgan (1688-1766), pioneer; the first white settler in the state; built a log cabin near Bunker Hill

ARCH A. MOORE, JR.

MATTHEW M. NEELY

MELVILLE D. POST

JENNINGS RANDOLPH

MARY LOU RETTON

Dwight Whitney Morrow (1873-1931), born in Huntington; lawyer, banker, diplomat; won the Distinguished Service Medal for his work during World War I; U.S. ambassador to Mexico during the Mexican-American crisis (1927-30); U.S. senator from New Jersey (1930-31)

Alfred Earl "Greasy" Neale (1891-1973), born in Parkersburg; professional baseball player, football coach; led all Cincinnati Reds hitters in the World Series against the Chicago "Black Sox" (1919); coached the Philadelphia Eagles to two football championships in the late 1940s; entered the Professional Football Hall of Fame (1967)

Matthew M. Neely (1874-1958), born in Fairmont; politician; U.S. representative (1913-20); U.S. senator (1922-40); governor of West Virginia (1941-45); pushed for labor and mining reforms that favored West Virginia residents

Christopher Harrison Payne (1848-1925), born near Red Sulphur Springs; clergyman, lawyer, federal official; West Virginia legislator (1896-98); U.S. Internal Revenue agent (1898-99); edited several newspapers that strengthened the black community; obtained passage of legislation for the West Virginia Colored Institute, now West Virginia State College

Francis H. Pierpont (1814-1899), born in Monongalia County; reformer, politician; opposed slavery and secession; governor of the restored government of Virginia at Wheeling (1861); governed western Virginia and helped form the independent state of West Virginia (1861-63)

Melville Davisson Post (1871-1930), born in Romines Mill; writer; wrote detective mysteries that some critics considered second only to those of Edgar Allan Poe; created the rural detective Uncle Abner; wrote *The Strange Schemes of Randolph Mason* and *Dwellers in the Hills*

Roger Price (1920-), born in Charleston; actor, artist; created "Droodles," simple drawings with comical captions

Jennings Randolph (1902-), born in Salem; politician; U.S. representative (1933-47); U.S. senator (1959-85); led the Senate Environment and Public Works committees for many years; created many public works projects and jobs while passing much air and water pollution legislation

Don Redman (1900-1964), born in Piedmont; composer, band leader; one of the first successful black orchestra leaders and jazz arrangers; starred in one of television's first black variety shows

Mary Lou Retton (1968-), born in Fairmont; gymnast; won the gold medal for all-around gymnastic performance in the 1984 Olympics, the first American gymnast to win a medal since 1948

Walter Reuther (1907-1970), born in Wheeling; labor leader; president of the United Automobile Workers (1946-70); president of the Congress of Industrial Organizations (CIO) (1952-55); negotiated welfare and pension plans and wage increases; in 1955, led the CIO to merge with American Federation of Labor (AFL)

John D. "Jay" Rockefeller IV (1937-   ), politician; moved to West Virginia in the 1960s to work in an antipoverty program; governor of West Virginia (1977-85); as governor, built roads, removed the sales tax on food, and recruited new industries to the state; U.S. senator (1985-   )

Andrew S. Rowan (1857-1943), born in Gap Mills; soldier; brought information to the United States from Cuban rebel leader Calixto Garcia y Iniquez during the Spanish-American War (1898), which inspired the story "A Message to Garcia"

Mary Lee Settle (1918-   ), born in Charleston; author; received the 1978 National Book Award for *Blood Tie*, which depicted expatriates in Turkey; wrote *The Kiss of Kin, Know Nothing, The Clam Shell*, and a four-volume novel based on West Virginia's history

Hubert Skidmore (1909-1946), born on Laurel Mountain; author; presented a realistic picture of mountain people in his writing; wrote *I Will Lift Up Mine Eyes*, which won the Jule Hopwood Prize (1936), and *Heaven Came So Near*

Harley O. Staggers (1907-   ), born in Keyser; politician; U.S. representative (1949-81); chaired the House Interstate and Foreign Commerce Committee

Lewis Strauss (1896-1974), born in Charleston; naval officer; directed the Atomic Energy Commission (1953-58); acting U.S. secretary of commerce (1958-59)

David Hunter Strother (1816-1888), born in Martinsburg; artist, author, soldier; illustrated *Blackwater Chronicles*; wrote for *Harper's New Monthly Magazine*; rose to the rank of brigadier general in the Union army

Cyrus Vance (1917-   ), born in Clarksburg; diplomat; represented President Lyndon B. Johnson in trouble spots such as Panama, Cyprus, and urban riot centers; negotiated the release of USS *Pueblo* and its crew; U.S. secretary of state (1977-81)

Booker T. Washington (1856-1915), grew up in Malden; educator, reformer; believed that blacks should work for education and employment rather than social equality with whites; founded Tuskegee Institute and the National Negro Business League; advocated cooperation between the races; wrote *Up From Slavery* (1901)

WALTER REUTHER

LEWIS STRAUSS

CYRUS VANCE

BOOKER T. WASHINGTON

HAROLD T. WEBSTER

CHUCK YEAGER

Harold Tucker Webster (1885-1952), born in Parkersburg; cartoonist; drew Caspar Milquetoast in "The Timid Soul" comic strip

Jerry West (1938-   ), born in Cabin Creek; professional basketball player; won all-American honors at West Virginia University; played for the Los Angeles Lakers; was the first player to score more than 4,000 playoff points; named to the National Basketball Association's all-time all-star team (1981)

Israel Charles White (1848-1927), born in Monongalia County; geologist; conducted a geological and economic survey of the state's natural resources; aided scientific oil development in Virginia and western Pennsylvania by formulating a theory for finding petroleum and gas deposits

William L. Wilson (1843-1900), born in Charles Town; politician; president of West Virginia University (1882-83); U.S. representative (1883-95); postmaster general (1895-97)

Charles E. "Chuck" Yeager (1923-   ), born in Myra; air force officer; the first pilot to break the sound barrier (1947)

Fielding Yost (1871-1946), born in Fairview; football coach; coached the University of Michigan's football teams (1901-27); directed the University of Michigan to the first Rose Bowl victory (1902); won ten Western Conference (now Big Ten) championships

GOVERNORS

Arthur I. Boreman	1863-1869	Homer A. Holt	1937-1941
Daniel D. T. Farnsworth	1869	Matthew Mansfield Neely	1941-1945
William E. Stevenson	1869-1871	Clarence W. Meadows	1945-1949
John J. Jacob	1871-1877	Okey L. Patteson	1949-1953
Henry M. Mathews	1877-1881	William C. Marland	1953-1957
Jacob B. Jackson	1881-1885	Cecil H. Underwood	1957-1961
Emanuel Willis Wilson	1885-1890	William Wallace Barron	1961-1965
Aretas Brooks Fleming	1890-1893	Hulett C. Smith	1965-1969
William A. MacCorkle	1893-1897	Arch A. Moore, Jr.	1969-1977
George W. Atkinson	1897-1901	John D. Rockefeller IV	1977-1985
Albert B. White	1901-1905	Arch A. Moore, Jr.	1985-1989
William M. O. Dawson	1905-1909	Gaston Caperton	1989-
William E. Glasscock	1909-1913		
Henry D. Hatfield	1913-1917		
John J. Cornwell	1917-1921		
Ephraim F. Morgan	1921-1925		
Howard M. Gore	1925-1929		
William G. Conley	1929-1933		
Herman Guy Kump	1933-1937		

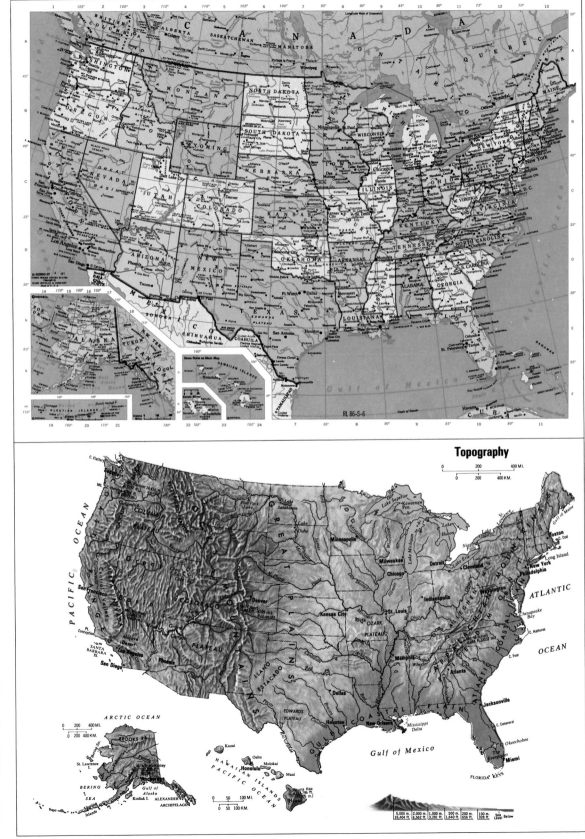

Topography

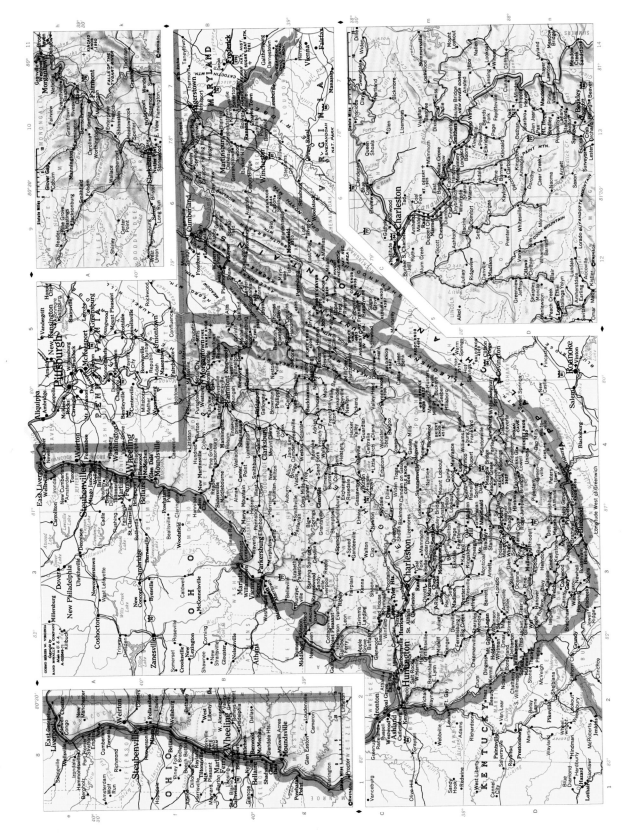

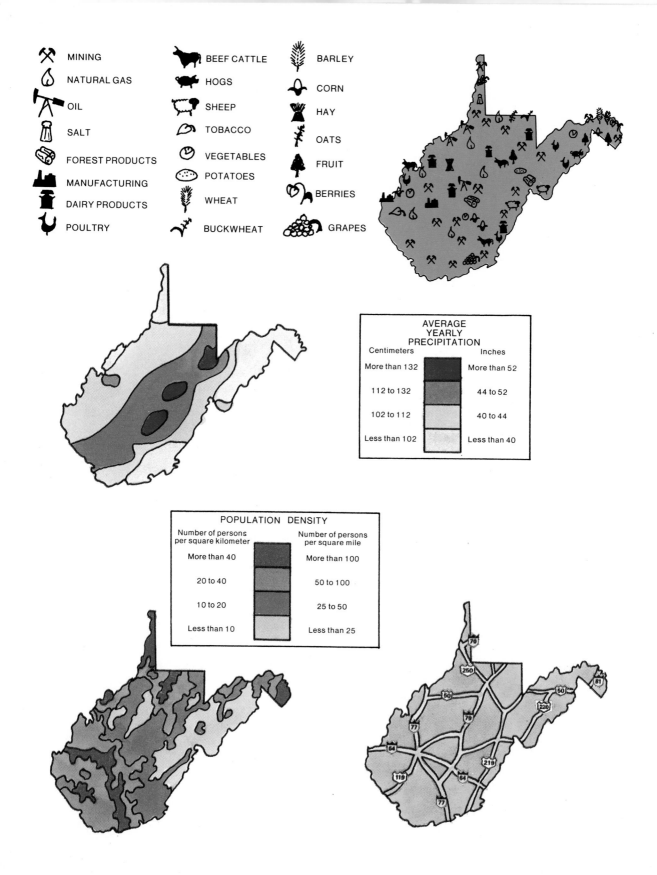

MINING

NATURAL GAS

OIL

SALT

FOREST PRODUCTS

MANUFACTURING

DAIRY PRODUCTS

POULTRY

BEEF CATTLE

HOGS

SHEEP

TOBACCO

VEGETABLES

POTATOES

WHEAT

BUCKWHEAT

BARLEY

CORN

HAY

OATS

FRUIT

BERRIES

GRAPES

AVERAGE
YEARLY
PRECIPITATION

Centimeters		Inches
More than 132		More than 52
112 to 132		44 to 52
102 to 112		40 to 44
Less than 102		Less than 40

POPULATION DENSITY

Number of persons per square kilometer		Number of persons per square mile
More than 40		More than 100
20 to 40		50 to 100
10 to 20		25 to 50
Less than 10		Less than 25

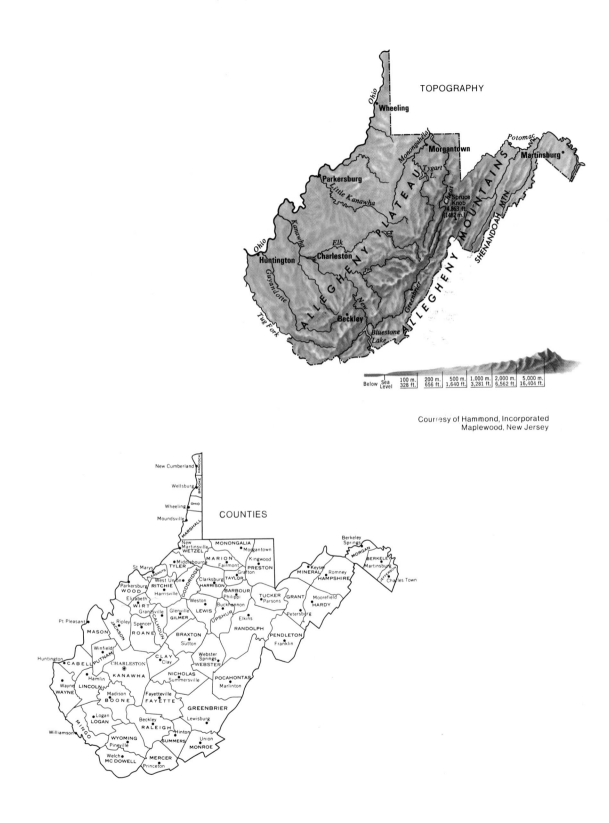

TOPOGRAPHY

Ohio

Wheeling

Morgantown

Potomac

Martinsburg

Monongahela

Tygart L.

Parkersburg

A L L E G H E N Y   P L A T E A U

Little Kanawha

Cheat

Spruce
Knob
4,863 ft.
(1482 m.)

A L L E G H E N Y   M O U N T A I N S

SHENANDOAH MTN.

Kanawha

Elk

Charleston

Ohio

Huntington

Guyandotte

New

Greenbrier

Beckley

Bluestone
Lake

Tug Fork

| Below Sea Level | 100 m. 328 ft. | 200 m. 656 ft. | 500 m. 1,640 ft. | 1,000 m. 3,281 ft. | 2,000 m. 6,562 ft. | 5,000 m. 16,404 ft. |

Courtesy of Hammond, Incorporated
Maplewood, New Jersey

COUNTIES

New Cumberland

HANCOCK
BROOKE

Wellsburg

Wheeling

OHIO

Moundsville

MARSHALL

New
Martinsville

Berkeley
Springs

MORGAN

WETZEL

MONONGALIA

Morgantown

BERKELEY

Martinsburg

St Marys

Middlebourne

MARION

Fairmont

PRESTON

Kingwood

MINERAL

Keyser

Romney

HAMPSHIRE

JEFFERSON

Charles Town

PLEASANTS

TYLER

West Union

DODDRIDGE

Clarksburg

TAYLOR

Grafton

Parkersburg

RITCHIE

Harrisville

HARRISON

BARBOUR

Philippi

TUCKER

Parsons

GRANT

Moorefield

WOOD

Elizabeth

WIRT

Grantsville

Glenville

Weston

Buckhannon

HARDY

LEWIS

UPSHUR

Petersburg

Pt Pleasant

Ripley

Spencer

GILMER

Elkins

MASON

JACKSON

CALHOUN

ROANE

BRAXTON

Sutton

RANDOLPH

PENDLETON

Franklin

Winfield

PUTNAM

CLAY

Clay

Webster
Springs

WEBSTER

POCAHONTAS

Marlinton

Huntington

CABELL

CHARLESTON

KANAWHA

NICHOLAS

Summersville

Hamlin

LINCOLN

Madison

Fayetteville

FAYETTE

Wayne

WAYNE

BOONE

GREENBRIER

Lewisburg

Logan

LOGAN

Beckley

RALEIGH

Hinton

Union

MONROE

Williamson

MINGO

WYOMING

Pineville

SUMMERS

Welch

MC DOWELL

MERCER

Princeton

Young people enjoying the Cacapon River on a summer day

INDEX

Page numbers that appear in boldface type indicate illustrations

139

A misty morning at sunrise near Flatwoods, in Braxton County

Picture Identifications

Front cover: Harpers Ferry
Back cover: Blackwater Falls, Blackwater Falls State Park
Pages 2-3: Rafters on the Tygart River, Undercut Rapid
Page 6: An autumn scene along Route 39, Nicholas County
Pages 8-9: The view from Homer Hamrick Point, east of Webster Springs
Pages 18-19: Montage of West Virginians
Pages 26-27: The restored kitchen of the Blennerhassett Mansion, originally built in 1798
Pages 40-41: A reenactment of the Civil War Battle of Droop Mountain, Droop Mountain Battlefield State Park
Pages 56-57: Early West Virginia coal miners
Page 72: The state capitol building, Charleston
Pages 80-81: Watoga State Park
Pages 92-93: The Glade Creek Grist Mill, in Babcock State Park
Page 108: Montage showing the state flag, state tree (sugar maple), state bird (cardinal), state flower (rhododendron), and state animal (black bear)

About the Author

R. Conrad Stein was born and grew up in Chicago. He graduated from the University of Illinois with a degree in history. Reading history books is Mr. Stein's hobby, and he tries to bring the excitement of history to the books he writes for young readers. The author lives in Chicago with his wife and their daughter Janna.

To prepare for writing this book, Mr. Stein traveled to West Virginia and toured the state. He was impressed by the marvelous scenery and the helpful people. He wishes especially to thank the staff of the State Museum in Charleston.